# GODS AND LITTLE FISHES

Senator Brookhart in Bucharest attired in the suit worn at diplomatic
dinners. The Senator yields the foreground of the picture to farming
compatriots of the eastern marches of Europe

# Gods and Little Fishes

*by*

ALFRED PEARCE DENNIS

ILLUSTRATED

THE BOBBS-MERRILL COMPANY

PUBLISHERS      INDIANAPOLIS

# CONTENTS

# ILLUSTRATIONS

# GODS AND LITTLE FISHES

# GODS AND LITTLE FISHES
## CHAPTER I
### INTRODUCTION

THE behaviorists will tell you that a man succeeds because it's implicit in his nature. He simply follows the larval instinct to struggle upward to the light. The lowly grub crawls out of the earth and becomes an iridescent-winged creature of the air. Thus it is that a man builds his success just as a robin instinctively fashions its nest.

The distinguished men I am writing about have this much in common—they must, through some imperious inner compulsion, struggle upward. What I am trying to do is to depict with camera-like precision tiny segments in their lives. I am not attempting biographies but rather episodes in individual careers. I am putting down in detail the impression certain distinguished men made upon me in the earlier and formative period of their lives. I write of them out of my own personal experience. What other people have thought or written about them plays no part in my narrative. A little man may come to sit at meat with big men and obscure men work with men of high distinction. It thus happens that the little man out of daily association may come to understand the big man. Countless little men have had Boswell's opportunity without Boswell's genius for making the most of it. The great Doctor Johnson himself remarks that biography is rarely well executed. "They only who live with a man can write his life with any genuine exactness and discrimination and few people who have lived with a man know what to remark about him." The writer has been privileged to know in their early days three men who later attained the presidency. What I have come to know of these and other distinguished men through personal association may or may not be worth setting down, but I am taking the chance on the general principle that the record which a mediocre man may make of the daily speech and behavior of a great man may sometimes serve as a valid and valuable human document. If George Washington's negro body-servant had possessed the wit to set down the daily orders which his master gave him he would have made a worth-while contribution to history. If we could procure a transcript of Lincoln's talk with the humblest of rustics it would be worth recording. Dean Inge remarks that if one of the apostles had had the gifts of Boswell we should probably have a rich collection of pregnant sayings of our Lord exhibiting wit and humor as well as gracious wisdom.

Some thirty years ago I knew Calvin Coolidge when as an obscure lawyer in Northampton, Massachusetts, he was making his début in politics as a candidate for city solicitor at a salary of eight hundred dollars per year. For four years on end we took our meals together at a modest hotel known as Rahar's Inn. At that time it never occurred to me that he might become a national, much less an international, figure and even to-day his rise to the highest pinnacle of political success is a miracle of miracles—more strange and confounding than cloven tongues, dried-up seas, or Aaron's rod that budded. I don't undertake to discuss his achievements but I clearly remember what we talked about as we sat in the small back room of Rahar's Inn. Mr. Coolidge, while never much on small talk, was not unwilling to talk about small things. One would find him solicitous about the health of Louie Dragon, one of the four Dragon brothers who kept a barber shop across the way. To Mr. Coolidge the health of a Northampton barber was not a trivial subject for conversation. It revealed the human sympathetic side of the man, and it was this human and sympathetic side which got him friends. Thus it was

It becomes more complex as it takes men out of the study, the laboratory, the cloister, into the great wrestling arena of life itself. Professor Wilson's iron will took him out of the classroom and into the White House with less than three years of actual political experience.

I write of Tarkington as a Princeton undergraduate. In college days before he had emerged from the common ruck of humanity he displayed a type of genius not unlike the many-sided personalities of the Italian Renaissance, such as Leon Battista Alberti, brilliant athlete, archer, mathematician, physicist, philosopher, man of letters, musician, sculptor, architect, portrait painter. The Tarkington I first knew seemed a delightful waster and slacker. To compose little verses on trivial subjects, to decorate sheets of paper with absurd drawings, to tinkle a guitar, to bicker ironically about unimportant matters, to rehearse for a college comedy, to indite an appropriate mot on a lady's fan—these were his serious academic employments. As Macaulay wrote of Horace Walpole, serious business was a trifle to him and trifles were his serious business. Nobody rated him as a serious writer. No one credited him with a hard, tough-fibered, invincible industry.

Of course every one now recognizes Mussolini

as an extraordinary genius, but we are wise after the event. I first had occasion to observe him just after the close of the war when serving the Department of Commerce as commercial attaché in the American Embassy at Rome. Mussolini, then a comparatively young man, displayed little talent for national leadership. He was a stormy petrel first coming into public notice at a time of great upheaval when horrible things were thrown to the surface. He was born, it would seem, to be an Ishmaelite, a non-conformist.

With one exception all the celebrities I write about possessed a quality in common: the quality of invincible industry, a sort of elemental creative instinct, a passion to get along, an urge to struggle upward to the heights. When it comes to this quality of invincible industry a person of the writer's mediocre capacity for work finds it difficult to evaluate a man like Mr. Hoover in terms of his own consciousness and experience. One may say of certain human beings, such as St. Paul, John Wesley, Balzac, Theodore Roosevelt, that they have been endowed with reservoirs of vital energy that are the admiration and despair of lesser men. Back of it all is a superabundant endowment of physical endurance, but the controlling factor in the equation is something we do not see—a spirit, a demon that drives and goads them. The great leader or pioneer is almost invariably a tragic personage. The ideas which he thinks to possess come to possess him. Spurred on by profound impatience with life he is dragged back and overwhelmed by that nameless thing which the physicists call inertia; which the political philosopher calls the power of the past, the accumulated wills and experiences of all who have gone before. The sparks that fly upward burn themselves out in the heights they crave. All human efforts, no matter how successful, end in final personal disaster. Death attends to that.

"Must I be carried to the skies on flowery beds of ease,
　While others fought to win the prize and sailed through bloody seas?"

No man of whom I write ever asked to be carried anywhere on flowery beds of ease. In some men, such as Ex-Labor-Secretary Davis, the will to work amounts to an endowment of genius. Some men are born tired and go through life tired—tired of work, tired of idleness, tired of boredom, tired of being tired. But if the Davises, Brookharts, Smoots of whom I write ever suffer from fatigue or boredom they keep the fact locked up within their own breasts.

What survives the dead hero? The true self of the man? Not at all, as seen through the mists of years. We remember a great king by the legend of burned cakes. Another hero by a cherry-tree myth. Another public servant by the trivial if not apocryphal jocosity: "What the country needs most is a good five-cent cigar." The scribbler pens the apothegm; the apothegm survives not only the scribbler but the true self of the hero. So it is that the veritable stature of the hero shrinks and shrivels to the phantom of an attitude. Time blurs the clear-cut lineaments of great men as we are swept remoteward on the heedless current of the years. Living men who toiled and aspired, working out their life wrestle on this planet, are soon swallowed up in oblivion, or if remembered at all, it is by some relic of a catch phrase—their memory attenuated to the phantom of an attitude or the echo of an echo. We sum up the many-sided, complex Woodrow Wilson in the label "idealist." Well, an ideal world is one without poverty, drunkenness, crime, police, noxious insects, zymotic diseases—where nobody works for money, nobody labors for hire. Professor Wilson impressed me not so much as an idealist as a born theorist, and his theories grew by what they fed upon. It is something to get at first hand the raw material that goes into the making of a hero's philosophy.

These men of whom I write toiled and struggled like men possessed. They were possessed. It's easy to say that a man is possessed with a desire to make money or become famous, but what possesses him after he has made a fortune or attained fame? Dostoyefsky classified Misha in *The Brothers Karamazoff* as "one of those who don't want millions but an answer to their questions." Such a type is Doctor Patton, former President of Princeton University, whose physical lassitude was only equaled by his intense intellectual activity—a man who did not care for fame or millions but who, pondering the mysteries of the universe, sought anxiously for an answer to his questions. What lay back of the pathetic epitaph on the tomb of the unknown Johannes who has lain for four centuries in an Italian cemetery:

"He who in life knew no rest, rests."

He has had enough of the fever of life; all he asks is surcease from toil and clamor; he wants nothing but peace and quiet.

One writing of successful men may be asked to define success. Success, I suppose, is getting what you want and being satisfied with it after you get it. Well, what are the qualities which insure a man getting what he wants and being satisfied with it after he has it? May not success or failure hinge on some absurd million-to-one chance—an irrelevance that may alter everything? How explain success and failure? Are some, according to the old Calvinistic theory, predestined to be saved and others to be lost? Given character, ability and industry, is success a matter of predictability just as in the exact science of astronomy an eclipse of the moon or the return of a comet is predictable? How far does luck or the indefinable quality called genius determine success? We say of a certain man that something is wrong with his luck. Either he has been in trouble or is in trouble or expects to be in trouble. An accidental illness may ruin the plans of a lifetime. All human beings totter on the edge of invisible hazard. Superficial thinkers appraise the success of a big man whom they can't otherwise explain in terms of luck. But is success over a period of years, whether in cards, love, the stock market, business, or in the learned professions a matter of luck? One heard a good deal about Lindbergh luck when he first blazed into fame. We now hear less about Lindbergh luck and more about Lindbergh's adequacy for his job.

Is success in politics a matter of playing the game

correctly? But what are the rules of the game? We have what might be called an industry of politics, but have we an art of politics; and if we have an art of politics, does there lie back of it a science of politics? Is there any systematized body of knowledge which a young man may master and infallibly become a successful politician, just as he may master the principles of medicine and become a successful practitioner? Is political success to be attained by direct seeking, or, as a by-product of something else, is it to be attained like happiness itself—indirectly? Politics is the art of carrying elections, and we say a man wins an election when he is more popular than his opponent. But what is the secret of popularity? In college it is fatal for a man to set out to make himself popular.

Of course a man can manufacture his own luck. One may say of Doctor Bratt, of whom I write, that he helped to create the sentiment in Sweden which later created him. Is the world filled with mute inglorious Miltons—men of native endowment and capacity who have failed because they lacked opportunity? In the matter of worldly success how far may we follow the Apostle Paul in his doctrine of salvation by grace? A quaint sixteenth-century theologian pushed the doctrine of salvation by grace to such an extreme as to conclude that good works are a positive detriment to salvation. Many a man is saved by the antecedent work of others. The glory of victory goes to the general rather than the men in the ranks who do the actual fighting. It takes a blind hero worshiper to subscribe to Carlyle's great-man theory of history. It may happen that the leader who exerts a pull upon his followers is also pushed by them. Most of the great discoveries and inventions represent the last link in a long chain of antecedent effort. The football player who takes the ball over the goal line for a touchdown scores as an individual, but his achievement is a last act in a series of composite efforts. The science of navigation had reached a point where the New World would have been discovered whether Columbus had lived or not. The pioneer breaks through the last barrier that divides the known from the unknown just as the last stroke of the miner's pick reveals the vein of ore at the bottom of the shaft. Adams and Leverrier, working along independent lines simultaneously discovered the planet Neptune. The science of astronomy had developed to such a point as to make the discovery of Neptune inevitable. The great man thus becomes the creature of circumstances because his achievement is rendered possible by the development of his particular art. Men thus become the products of their milieu. While a modern American satirist might duplicate Swift's *Gulliver's Travels* no poet of to-day could write *Paradise Lost* any more than the modern painter could reproduce the ethereal, angelic faces that smile from the canvases of Andrea del Sarto and Fra Angelico. The naïve, childlike faith of the fifteenth-century devotional painters inspired their work. They were a product of their own particular age. I write that Mr. Coolidge's plainness of speech and unaffectedness of behavior made him intelligible to the mass mind. The average man is able to dramatize himself in Mr. Coolidge because most of us are not brilliant. Mr. Coolidge's great popularity was due in no small measure to the inferiority consciousness of millions of small-minded people to whom Mr. Coolidge made himself intelligible by coming down to their level. It would be hard for the average man to dramatize himself in the poet Shelley. As an idealist he stands too far below Shelley; as a realist too far above him. Van Buren, Polk, Buchanan, Pierce were second-raters as compared with Clay, Calhoun, Webster, Blaine, but they succeeded where the more brilliant man failed. The craving of the American people is not for a brilliant man, but for a safe man in the White House. Mr. Roosevelt, whose restless genius kept him in a ferment of activity, would have taken the first train South when the Mississippi River broke its bounds. Mr. Wilson, a more intellectual man than Mr. Coolidge, embarked on an overseas expedition for the purpose of setting aright the affairs of the Old World. It is safe to say that Mr. Coolidge in like circumstances would not have budged from the White House. As to the Mississippi floods, he served the country better by remaining at home and deputizing Mr. Hoover, who specializes in floods and famines. These big men of whom I write are neither supermen, geniuses, nor, like the salmon, blind sports of nature. They are neither gods nor little fishes.

# CHAPTER II

### THE EUROPEAN EDUCATION OF SENATOR BROOKHART, ALONG WITH THE SENATORIAL REPLY

SENATOR SMITH WILDMAN BROOKHART, of Iowa, was born in a Missouri log cabin, knew the vicissitudes of life as a dirt-farmer boy and, having migrated to Iowa, practised law for thirty years in Washington, a town of less than five thousand inhabitants. Some chronicler will find strong meat in the story of Mr. Brookhart's translation from Washington, Iowa, to Washington, District of Columbia. But that is not my job. I can only contribute from first-hand experience, and my experience has to do with Mr. Brookhart in full bloom rather than in the bud.

As everybody knows, Mr. Brookhart began his political career as a petty henchman of Senator Cummings. He later differed with Cummings on railroad policies. But as Senator Cummings hardened into a conservative, Mr. Brookhart, the cowhide radical, broke with him and finally defeated him. Cummings had the satisfaction of denouncing Brookhart as an economic illiterate, and Brookhart had the satisfaction of beating Cummings at the polls by seventy-two thousand majority. Mr. Brookhart may thus be compared to a vigorous young plant which, thrusting its roots into the crevices of an ancient stone wall, overthrows it.

As a plain man of the people, it was not enough to be named Smith—Wildman had to be tacked on to it. As scions of the blood royal are expected to live up to their princely attributes, so Commoner Brookhart, the radical, has consistently lived up to the expectations implied in the baptismal name "Smith Wildman."

He got some education in the Iowa country schools. A distant cousin, John Grinstead, taught him that a man can learn more out of school than in school. Like college professors, Mr. Brookhart educates himself through the process of educating others. The education received from one's fellows is like the mysterious law of endosmosis and exosmosis in chemistry, by which two liquids separated from each other by a partition flow through the barrier and intermingle.

To educate and to be educated—that is Mr. Brookhart's great purpose in life. He is skeptical about the old order. People must be educated out of their easy acceptances and compliances. The radical looks forward rather than backward. For him, this changing world is continually unfolding. For the radical, life is one perpetual offensive and defensive campaign against reactionaries and stand-patters. Radicalism is only another name for the skepticism which is the precursor of all progress. Men who are perfectly content with the existing order never make any progress. A crab grows by bursting its hard shell and casting it off. Mr. Brookhart is goaded on in his educational mission just as was Ciriaco of Ancona in the days of the Italian revival of learning. "I go," cried he, "to awake the dead!"

Homer speaks of the sea as the estranging main. Crossing the sea is the best of educators. Early in the summer of 1923 Senator Brookhart journeyed to Europe "to exchange views with the leaders over there." In the free-for-all discussions which followed, both sides stood to profit. The great, intangible values of life are, of course, incapable of mathematical expression, but certain features of the Senator's European trip may be envisaged statistically.

Countries visited—fifteen.

Time occupied in traipsing over Europe—eight weeks.

Chancellors, ministers of state, men of commerce, statistical sharks and rifle-shooters interviewed—some two hundred odd.

Royal palaces, castles, picture galleries, cathedrals inspected—none.

Dance-halls, cabarets, cafés, theaters, cinema houses frequented—none.

Baggage transported, trunks, suitcases, portmanteaus, steamer rugs—none. (The Senator, as the saying goes, traveled light, with one small bag.)

Language employed by the Senator in all foreign countries—American.

European *objets d'art*, bibelots, kinkajous purchased—none.

Printed information gathered—six or eight mail sacks.

Wines, beers, spirituous liquors, including absinth, cognac, vodka, consumed—not a chemical trace.

Illustrated postal cards sent back home—none.

Pictures of Westminster Abbey, The Lion of Lucerne, The Colosseum, The Brandenburger Thor, The Tomb of Napoleon purchased—none.

My knowledge of these details is based on hard, vivid, first-hand experience. I had been serving in Europe for some five or six years as commercial attaché in such embassy posts as Rome and London, and later as an itinerant economic investigator for Mr. Hoover, Secretary of Commerce. I happened to be at Vienna when instructed by cable to meet Senator Brookhart on his arrival at Cherbourg and assist him in working out plans for his European tour.

On arrival he was unattended by porters, unencumbered by heavy luggage, and as lightly equipped sartorially as if he were journeying from Bloomfield, Iowa, to attend a Grangers' picnic at the neighboring town of Keosauqua. The Senator was as light in his Baedeker preparation for Europe as he was in his baggage. He expected to find the summer climate of northern Europe no different from that of Iowa. "Folks are just folks, anywhere you find them," he was wont to observe, and it was annoying to run across idiosyncrasies in dress, language, railroad transportation and monetary symbols. I see him holding in his pudgy palm a scrambled lot of paper marks, francs, kronen, lei or rubles, and inquiring incredulously, "What is this stuff worth in real money?"

It being summer-time, the Senator had left his overcoat done up in moth-balls at home. He suffered from cold, and things grew worse as we crossed the Channel to England, worked north into Scotland, and later crossed the North Sea into the Scandinavian countries. In chilly Edinburgh I lent him my overcoat. He wore it for five weeks straight, until one sunny morning, walking along the Calea Victorei, Bucharest, Rumania, he handed

Senator Brookhart clad in the author's overcoat along with the coatless
author amid the summer snows of Norway

it back to me with the remark, "Now we are getting back to a decent summer climate like we have at home, I guess I can make out without an overcoat."

In later years the Senator disappointed me by voting against the elastic provisions of the tariff, but elasticity does have its advantages in the case of overcoats. The Senator's breadth of shoulder and girth surpassed my own by at least ten inches and his weight mine by some sixty pounds, but the coat, made on the accordion-pleated plan, possessed elastic properties which served fully to encompass the senatorial figure. But the overcoat, like the flexible tariff, could be successfully worked for increases and not for decreases. In point of readaptation of the coat to the figure of the owner, it was a case of a big shuck to a mighty small ear of corn.

We spent the first evening in Paris in a hotel room listening to the Senator's exposition of the Rochdale cooperative experiment. In early life Mr. Brookhart had "read up" on the Rochdale cooperative movement. The system was worked out a century ago by the weavers of Rochdale, England, and represents an attempt, through cooperative buying and selling, to eliminate the middleman in merchandising transactions.

The next morning, while waiting in the ante-room of the American Embassy to be received by Mr. Herrick, I ran across an old friend, Mr. Alba Johnson, former president of the Baldwin Loco-motive Works. Learning why I had come to Paris, Mr. Johnson expressed a desire to meet "that wild man," as he called Senator Brookhart. He seemed to regard Mr. Brookhart as some sort of anthro-pological curio, such as a leaf wearer of Orissa or a pigmy from the forests of the Belgian Congo.

Making known to Mr. Brookhart that Mr. John-son would be pleased to make his acquaintance, the Senator gracefully acceded: "Well, I won't re-fuse to shake hands with any American in a foreign country, I don't care who he is."

The greetings as between countrymen were as follows:

Mr. Johnson: "So you're Senator Brookhart, of Iowa?"

The Senator: "And ain't you the Mr. Johnson who's been connected with the Association of Rail-road Manufacturers?"

"Yes," replied Mr. Johnson, drawing himself up proudly, glad to be identified as a man of affairs, "I've long been an officer in the association."

"Well, Mr. Johnson," pursued the Senator, "all I can say is that you're an officer in one of the most iniquitous, nee-far-ious outfits in the entire country. You take excess profits from the railroads in furnishing their supplies and they take it from the farmers in excess rates."

That terminated the interview.

It was unfortunate that the blameless Mr. Johnson had been identified with one of the Senator's taboos. From the beginning of his political career the Senator had jousted freely with the railroads. According to him the railroads had been no friend to his friends—the farmers and other toilers. The Senator's mind, particularly in his earlier days, was a great deal like that of the primitive man, tattooed over with monstrous images. Typical monstrous images tattooed on the Senator's mind are Wall Street, the railroads, high society, combinations, international bankers, and the nearer you get to them the worse they seem.

If the primitive man is affrighted by his taboos he is comforted by faith in his fetishes. The Senator's pet fetishes are agricultural cooperation, the Volstead Act, the Rochdale experiment, the export debenture, more pay for the poor out of the pockets of the rich, the magic power of government to transmute leaden instincts into golden conduct. He is always for the unorganized man as against protected industry.

[ 33 ]

The Senator was charmed with Ambassador Herrick, who had unconsciously prepared for this delightful rencounter by providentially writing a book on the cooperative movement some three or four years before.

That evening we again sat in a hotel room and discussed the Rochdale cooperatives. Then came a round of official calls. It was a lean day that did not yield interviews with a dozen French functionaries. As a side diversion I arranged a call upon Monsieur Menier, the big chocolate manufacturer. A superserviceable lackey at the door demanded our cards.

"But I've never had any visiting cards printed," exclaimed the Senator.

As a substitute he inscribed in pencil on a piece of paper, "Senator Brookhart, of Iowa, U. S. A." Now, the average Frenchman is an odd fish who quaintly writes roast beef "rosbif" and takes liberties even with the alphabet. Who but a Frenchman would convert the good old vowel *i* into *j* and then turn around and pronounce the *j* as if it were a *y*, and use *v* in the place of our *w*? Thus the impulsive Menier, advancing to meet his distinguished guest and reading from the improvised card,

## Senator Brookhart
### of
## Iowa, U. S. A.

rolled out:

"*Enchanté de vous voir, M'sieur le Senateur Brook-a-r-r-r-r de Yovah.*"

The Senator, dumfounded at hearing his name rolled out like the roar of a machine-gun, turned to me in an aside and inquired,

"What's he talking about Jehovah for?"

No wonder the Senator couldn't get it out of his head that the French are a decadent people. One evening I got him to adjourn the discussion of the Rochdale experiment for a stroll on the grand boulevards, pleading the need of exercise, though goodness knows I needed no exercise at night after running around with him all day. Crowds of people were seated around little tables on the broad sidewalks of the Boulevard des Italiens. A happy, pleasure-loving throng, enjoying the soft June evening, sipping bock, sirup, *apéritifs,* puffing cigarettes, gossiping, ogling the passers-by.

"These people are bound straight for perdition," commented the Senator judicially. "The drinking is even worse than I expected."

A delicious strain of music floated from a dancing pavilion.

[ 35 ]

"Let's go in and have some refreshment and watch the people dance," I suggested.

"No," replied the Senator grimly, "I don't dance; I make other people dance."

The Senator doesn't drink, dance, smoke, play cards, cuss, tell shady stories. Mr. Brookhart in five days had exhausted Paris and had exhausted me. I had expected to return to Vienna after heading the Senator for England. But this was not to be. He had cabled Mr. Hoover that the success of his mission depended upon my continued attendance. My orders came to stand by the Senator as long as needed. I had already come to admire and respect Mr. Brookhart, and he interested me greatly as a human being filled with courage and devotion, and without a particle of pose or affectation. As Carlyle said of Sterling, "Despite many unsuitable wrappages of Church-of-Englandism and other, my heart loved the man."

I had been hopping from one European country to another for the better part of six years, but could even the most efficient grasshopper be expected to keep pace with the Graf Zeppelin? Could any ordinary mortal stand the pace? Could tired nature hold out? Luckily I had friends among American officials in the European capitals. These kind people "spelled" me. I make particularly grateful recognition of the services of the following: Hugh Butler, American trade commissioner in London, Harry Sorensen, American trade commissioner at Copenhagen, Colonel Haskell, of the Hoover Relief Organization in Russia, Admiral Bristol, commander of our destroyer fleet in Turkish waters, Julian Gillespie, American commercial attaché at Constantinople, Margaret Goldsmith, American trade commissioner at Berlin, Leopold Kotnowski, secretary of the Polish-American Chamber of Commerce at Warsaw. Above all, Elizabeth Humes, now American trade commissioner at Rome. As translator, interpreter, liaison officer and sympathetic listener, Miss Humes' services were perfect beyond qualification or reservation. We cleaned up Paris in five days, but we left for England without seeing the Louvre, the Invalides, Notre Dame, the Arc de Triomphe, Montmartre, Versailles or Fontainebleau. Like the peasant hero of Gustave Nadaud's poem, "he never gazed on Carcassonne."

We arrived in London on the evening of July third, and the next day called at the British Foreign Office for the purpose of "ascertaining what the British Government is going to do about Russia."

Ushered into the august presence of an under-

[ 37 ]

secretary, ruddy of countenance, of the riding-to-hounds type as depicted in novels of British high life, the Senator came directly to the point:

"Now, Mr. Secretary, what are you people going to do about Russia? Russia is up and coming, and it looks to me like we ought to recognize the Russian Government."

"But, Senator, you must remember that the Soviet Government has confiscated millions of pounds sterling of British property, and until restitution is made, how can we be expected to treat them as if nothing of the kind had occurred? Furthermore, you must remember that the present Soviet régime is a revolutionary government. Do you expect us to condone revolution?"

"Well," drawled the Senator, "I like their government all the better for that reason. We have no prejudice against revolutions. We called on the Mexican revolutionists to overthrow Maximilian, one of the breed of potentates sent over by Europe to rule the poor Mexicans. Later we supported the revolutionists in Cuba. Again, our President Wilson called on the German people to rise and overthrow their monarchical government. And, Mr. Secretary, though you may not be aware of it, to-day is the fourth day of July, or the anniversary of the greatest revolutionary doctrine ever promulgated. I mean the throwing off the yoke of your King George III." There was nothing more to be said.

Senator Brookhart, though not a deep student of ancient and medieval history, displayed a positive genius for setting the British officials to rights on matters of modern historic import.

When in Copenhagen, the American Minister, Mr. Prince, most ceremonious of manner and all a-flutter in top hat and frock coat and light-colored spats, escorted the Senator over to meet a British savant cited by Mr. Prince as an authority on all things Danish. The gentleman in question, as every British schoolboy knows, springs from a long line of blue-blooded ancestors, with a country estate which may be identified for present purposes as Wormwood Coppice, Outgrowlers Heath, Bury St. Omans, Hants. Senator Brookhart took the whole affair as an informal gathering of farmers at a meeting of the state Grange, and immediately began a eulogy of the perfections of the Danish agricultural cooperatives. The British encyclopedist broke in by exclaiming:

"Well, really, we don't have cooperative organizations in England, you know."

"Is it possible," inquired the Senator, "that you have never heard of the Rochdale cooperatives?

In my opinion, the biggest thing that is going on in England to-day is the cooperative movement, and you are one man who doesn't know anything about it!"

We proceeded from London to Edinburgh to attend a convention of British cooperatives. I contrived to have an invitation conveyed to the Senator to address the gathering. His theme was the human parasites which suck the blood out of the hard-working producers. He developed his subject without heat, without gesticulation, pressing forward to his peroration with all the inexorable logic of the cosmic process:

"Take our American railroads; at least seven billion dollars of their capitalization is pure water, but our roads are run in the interest of Wall Street, and Wall Street must have dividends on this watered stock. That means that the American farmer must pay heavy toll to Wall Street every time he ships a bushel of wheat or a yearling calf to market. Of course the answer to this is to organize our buying and selling cooperatively, and to cut our transportation charges in half by running the railroads in the interest of the general public rather than of Wall Street."

The Senator's speech went over big. He got a tremendous hand. Perhaps this was the most felicific episode of the entire trip, unless it was the experience of being piped on board an American destroyer lying in the Black Sea off the harbor of Odessa and served at dinner with a chicken pie "à la Iowa."

We crossed from Newcastle, England, to Bergen, Norway, and in pursuit of information attained Finse on the lofty Norwegian plateau. With the ground covered by six feet of snow in July, what I most needed was not information but an overcoat. We fetched a compass round by Stockholm to Denmark and there inspected cooperative packing houses, cooperative dairies, and the last word of excellence in Danish hog pens. The Danish agricultural co-ops furnished the Senator intellectual pasturage as rich as the lush meadows of clover and alfalfa upon which thousands of thoroughbred Danish cattle were grazing.

We got off to a good start in Berlin. I had covered the ground in Germany and Poland a short time before with Mr. William Butterworth, later president of the United States Chamber of Commerce, whose hunger for information was almost as unappeasable as Mr. Brookhart's. During the first day in Berlin we interviewed the chief of the Social Democratic Labor Party, a director of the Reichsbank, a *Geheimrat* in the Raiffeisen Bank for credit to farmers, a commissar in the Russian Soviet Purchasing Office, a *Herr Doktor* in the Potash Syndicate, with a peep at the Reichstag in session and a formal call upon Chancellor Cuno. Here again we were up against outworn conventions of the Old World, with a doorman demanding the Senator's card for presentation to the Chancellor. A piece of paper had to be found on which the Senator inscribed, without calligraphic recreations, his name. The transmittal of this scrap of paper to the German Chancellor obviously recalled the association of scraps of paper with German Chancellors. On the whole, we did better in Berlin than in Paris, where the Senator missed his date with Poincaré while at the battle-field of Château-Thierry. Mr. Brookhart, however, displayed an amiable philosophy about this contretemps.

"Well," he remarked, "I guess Poncarey has missed just as much in not getting my views as I have missed in not receiving his."

Mr. Brookhart much enjoyed an exchange of views with a *hochwohlgeboren* marksman of a local *Schützen Verein.* Be it known that Senator Brookhart rose from a humble start in a log cabin to become one of the world's best rifle trainers and rendered great service during the war instructing our young soldiers in the art of straight shooting. Pointing to a tree about thirty meters tall, standing in the park, the German marksman put this question:

"From the extreme summit of that tree so lofty could your *Excellenz* with a rifle a small squirrel shoot *aus?*"

"Yes," replied the Senator modestly, "I could easily shoot the animal through the head at that distance."

We reaped a harvest in Poland, doing the country in the grand manner, assisted by the indefatigable Kotnowski, secretary of the Polish-American Chamber of Commerce. Stores of information amassed had to do with: agricultural syndicates, cooperative trading associations, parcellation of the great landed estates, the constitution and activity of the State Agrarian Bank, the index of wholesale prices in zloties, the great lumber resources of the Miedzyrzecze Forest, the Polish budget figures, balance sheet of the Polski Bank, the match monopoly, plans for the construction of the Polish port of Gdynia, reports on the beet-sugar crop, export and import statistics, reports of the Minister of Finance and the Minister of Commerce, laws dealing with factory inspection, unemployment, labor unions, national health-insurance schemes, the

housing situation, reconstruction of devastated
areas. We looked into the work of a prominent
cooperator, Dr. Franciszek Stefczyk, who founded
the first Polish Bank on the German Raiffeisen principle, and examined with approval the flourishing
condition of the Polish cooperative societies at
Lwów. (This Polish name for the metropolis of
Galicia is effectually pronounced by barking it,
just as the city of Tczew may be vocalized by
sneezing it and the famed city of Przemysl best
handled by gargling it along with an infusion of
slippery-elm bark.)

Thus we gathered up our material as wandering
woolly sheep collect cockleburs. Our printed stores,
whether in German, Polish, Danish or French—
none of these languages being understood by the
Senator—were bundled into diplomatic pouches
and dispatched to the Senate Office Building in
Washington, where they repose undisturbed. Art
is long and time is fleeting. The pressure of the
current hour displaces the great matters of the
past, postponed for consideration to a future date
which never comes. A busy life with little time
left to count the stars, the birds, the fishes, or to
admire Italian Renaissance paintings or to taste
the savor of the polished periods of Walter Pater
and Edmund Burke. One day the Senator is bent

on getting better salaries for government clerks, another time it's cleaning up patronage jobbery in the South, then again it's more pay for disabled veterans or a larger appropriation for the Farm Board. So much time to be spent in harassing the regular Republicans, resenting his classification as a "pseudo-Republican"—will the time ever come for digesting all that European stuff? As a result of many interruptions, the Senator's purpose to tell the whole story has been frustrated, and he can only say, with the prophet: "As thy servant was busy here and there, he was gone."

The Senator crossed the Russian frontier with emotions of deep and sympathetic interest for the Russian people and their new experiment in government and economics. The Senator's admiration for the Soviet Government is understandable, since he shares the Russian infatuation that government can do anything and care for everybody. A man of rude, half-starved beginnings who had become newly enfranchised and charged with the complex responsibilities of administration would, of course, be drawn toward millions of unenfranchised peasants who had now come into their own. Voltaire maintains that government exists for the purpose of taking money out of one man's pocket and putting it into another man's pocket. Some

ground for Voltaire's theory existed in the days of
the old French monarchy, with a politico-economic
system based on privilege. Senator Brookhart's
political theory is more constructive. On the negative side he would prevent government from taking
money out of any man's pocket for the benefit of
another. On the positive side he would have government put money into everybody's pocket.
"Special privileges for none," thundered Colonel
Bryan. "General privileges for everybody," demands Senator Brookhart. He would double the
appropriation for the control of the Mississippi;
he would triple the half billion Farm Board appropriation; he would set rediscount rates by
statute and abolish poverty by government edict.
His program would be something like laying out
a railroad in a rough country where the hills are
scraped down to level up the valleys. According
to the Senator, his Iowa farmer friends had suffered
with the Russian peasants in kind if not in degree
through the arrogant exactions of overlords. Here
is a story of social injustice which he narrates:

In the summer of 1920 two Wall Street magnates were strolling up Broadway. One turned
to the other and remarked, "Well, I guess it's about
time we deflate the farmer." So they turned the
thumbscrews of credit on the unfortunate farmer

and in the general deflation hundreds of thousands were driven into bankruptcy, with the market value of Iowa farms cut in half and mortgages plastered over the land—all due to a sudden whim that had occurred to one of the financial magnates of Wall Street.

He will talk to you by the hour of the consumers' strike, the wholesale cancellation of orders, the almost instantaneous vertical drop in staple farm products. By fatal chance, a vertical increase in freight rates coincided almost to a day with the vertical drop in the price of farm products. The increase in freight rates is laid by him at the door of the Esch-Cummings Transportation Act. It looked like discrimination against the farmer. In times of adversity primitive men of simple faiths people the universe with malevolent agents who have to be prayed to and propitiated. The disappointed, defeated man, brooding over his troubles, surrenders to the hallucination that he is the victim of a conspiracy to down him. This is the familiar delusion of persecution. It is human nature to charge up misfortunes to some one else's caprice, selfishness or malevolence. A man strikes his shins against a chair in the dark and curses not himself but the chair. Thus it is that Mr. Brookhart comes dangerously near at times to making a profession out of human discontent. But why not? Without discontent there is no progress in the world, and many professions, such as that of doctor or dentist, are built on an effort to alleviate the individual's discontent with himself.

If there is pain in the social tissue, Mr. Brookhart is for relieving it at once, just as a dentist would relieve a toothache by wrenching out the tooth. When evil appears "something ought to be done about it." This means a passion for instant action. Thus it is that many good people come to believe that they will most benefit the world when they most relieve their own feelings. As Walter Bagehot points out, the literary theory of the British constitution—for example, as Blackstone describes it—is quite a different thing from the actual working of the British constitution. So of Russia. Even by 1923 the paper communistic theory of the Soviet régime had long since lagged behind the actualities of administration. The doctrines of Lenin had become something to be declaimed by rather than to live by. Lenin had already begun to swing over to a cooperative movement, and that pleased the Senator. Communism was accepted as is a vague theological dogma to which we render lip service rather than actual obedience. The old manorial estates had been

[ 48 ]

seized and divided among the peasants, with the land held in small parcels by squatters' rights. These rights are likely to endure until the last crack of doom. The peasants having obtained what they most wanted—the land—were tolerably satisfied, and this satisfaction the Senator attributed to the beneficence of the Soviet régime. The Russian peasant is an apathetic clod with a fatalistic philosophy of life. His blessed word *"Nichevo"* may be variously interpreted, "Why worry?" "What's the use?" Ask him what the communists are doing in Moscow.

"How does that concern me?" he replies. *"Nichevo! Nichevo!* Why should I bother? We have our village and have divided among ourselves the soil of the great landowners. Why bother about what the government is doing?"

As the Russian peasants are fairly well satisfied and as they constitute eighty-five per cent. of the population, no doubt the Senator is right in his conclusion that the Russian people have profited by the revolution and are far happier than under the old Czarist régime. There are some who do not accept the utilitarian doctrine of the greatest happiness to the greatest number as a justification for inflicting wrongs upon the minority. But at any rate, Mr. Brookhart went into Russia expecting to see a regenerated Russia. He saw what he expected to see; rather, what he wanted to see. He was determined to be pleased. He even went so far as to accept an invitation from Colonel Haskell to attend a grand-opera performance in Moscow. The lengths to which he will go to indulge a friend is one of the secrets of the Senator's political success. At any rate, he accepted the Russian opera in the same spirit of acquiescent fortitude that his Soviet comrades might politely have displayed at an Iowa hog-calling contest.

The leveling process on the social side did not fail to carry its appeal to the Senator. Mr. Brookhart is not strong on social distinctions. To him they are vanity of vanities. Washington hostesses on the lookout for rough diamonds found in the Senator an appeal to their collector's passion for the rare and unattainable. But he is indifferent to social preferment.

The Senator regards the social lobby as the most insidious of all the lobbies, but even the wariest bird gets caught sometimes. In December, 1926, Mr. Brookhart was invited to a big dinner at the Willard Hotel in Washington. He threw the invitation in a waste-basket, but when assured by another Senator that it was from a friend of the Progressive group, he went. He found himself

Summer styles of 1923, representing Rumania, Paris and Iowa

placed at the table between Otto Kahn, of Kuhn, Loeb & Co., and E. E. Loomis, of the House of Morgan, and, as the Senator tells it, was the only man there dressed like an American citizen. Mr. Kahn began to expostulate with the Senator over his plan to squeeze the water out of the railroads and to set rediscount rates by statute. Mr. Loomis followed suit. Meanwhile hip-pocket flasks had been exposed at another table to the view of the Senator. Here were his three pet detestations—high society, Wall Street and booze—commingled. When the dinner was breaking up, some one inquired:

"Senator, did you feel contaminated by having Kuhn, Loeb & Co. on one side of you and the House of Morgan on the other?"

"I might have been infected," he replied dryly, "but for the fact that I had been inoculated against the contagion."

In southern Russia, Mr. Brookhart, who carries the Fourth of July with him, and with it an American investiture of everything foreign, found himself much at home. Here was a fertile zone almost indistinguishable from the rich black soil of Iowa, extending from the Carpathian Mountains, as if laid on with a huge paint brush, across Bessarabia, sweeping eastward beyond the Volga

[ 51 ]

River, around the southern slopes of the Urals, and then stretching away into Siberia to the Altai Mountains in central Asia. Mr. Brookhart emerged from Russia by way of Odessa, and through the courtesy of Admiral Bristol was taken by an American destroyer to Constantinople and later back to the Rumanian port of Constantza.

On arrival at Bucharest I made shift, while Mr. Brookhart was occupied with a caller, to post over to the American Legation and apprise our Minister, Peter Augustus Jay, of the Senator's advent. I had served in the Rome Embassy with my friend Jay, and made bold to suggest that he invite the Senator for luncheon and not for dinner. I explained that Mr. Brookhart had come to Europe with only one suit of clothes, which served as a covering but not as an ornament to the body. I quoted Mr. Brookhart's sartorial platform as enunciated on a public occasion:

"I never wore a swallowtail, never owned one, and never will admit the necessity for such a uniform."

I also mentioned Mr. Brookhart's antipathy to wine, coffee and tobacco, and his contempt for the ceremonials which surround a formal dinner.

"But why," Mr. Jay asked, "should I attempt to accommodate myself to Senator Brookhart's way of living any more than he should accommodate himself to my way of living? Please ask the Senator to come around here and take dinner with us at eight o'clock."

It would be hard to imagine two men whose lives presented wider contrasts. Mr. Brookhart with his humble beginnings and early merciless buffetings, blunt of speech, unschooled in the ways of diplomacy, all contrasting with Jay's upbringing. Jay, born to the purple, standing six feet two inches in height, grandson of the great John Jay, Harvard graduate, for twenty years a member of the Diplomatic Corps, rich enough to buy up ten sections of Iowa farm lands. Mr. Brookhart's knowledge of horses was obtained empirically in guiding a plow behind a pair of farm plugs. Jay's knowledge was obtained didactically under the instruction of a riding master, keeping in his stables at Bucharest not less than nine saddle horses. Mr. Brookhart and Mr. Jay looked at life from different angles, just as they had looked at a horse from different angles.

Be all this as it may, we punctually appeared at Minister Jay's for the eight o'clock dinner. Mr. Brookhart, wearing a spotless celluloid collar and a pepper-and-salt suit which had gone unpressed for six weeks, was welcomed by Mr. Jay and his two secretaries, the three resplendent in evening dress.

Straightway a flunky appeared, bearing cocktails on a silver platter. The Senator employed the characteristic straight-armed, blocking-off movement of a running halfback on a football field.

"Take that away. I never touch the stuff," he objected decisively.

Mr. Brookhart is no modest violet, and seated at the right of the Minister at dinner, he comfortably squared himself, hitched up his coat sleeves an inch or two and started in to tell all about the "European situation."

"You people in high society," he observed, "know what the aristocrats are doing, but you don't know what's really going on over here, because you don't know what the common people are doing."

"Indeed," inquired Mr. Jay politely, "and what are the common people doing?"

"Well, let me tell you. First I will give you an insight into that great country, Russia, in which I spent the better part of three weeks. These Russians are up and coming. In many respects they are way ahead of us."

"In what respects?" inquired Mr. Jay.

"Well, they're long-headed financiers, for instance."

"You mean that they are long-headed about seizing the property of Americans and giving them a receipt for it, written on a worthless piece of paper? Is that what you mean by long-headed financiers?"

"You are prejudiced," countered the Senator, "because you haven't been in there. You don't understand the situation. You take Trotzky, for example. I had a long conference with Trotzky. I came away with the impression that he is a greater financial genius than our Paul Warburg."

By this time the harassed Jay was in a position to concede the point. He reached over indulgently, patted the Senator on the shoulder, and remarked:

"I dare say, Senator, your friend Trotzky is a very delightful gentleman."

I had displayed an incredible lack of judgment in feeling that a meeting between two men who stood so far apart in their philosophies of life would break up with a stiff quarrel and hard feelings on both sides. As the evening wore on our Minister and our Senator became actually clubby with each other, each one being interested in the other as he would be in some sport of nature. It was the charm of the unusual, like running across a zebra in a watermelon patch.

Driving home that night in a rattletrap *caléche* drawn by a mangy little pony, my companion remained silent until we were approaching our hotel. My thoughts were on my friend Jay. His splendid establishment, his magnificent stable, his munificence in presenting an admired thoroughbred to Queen Marie.

"Your friend Jay," remarked the Senator, "has qualities about him I like, and I guess at bottom he's a pretty good sort of a fellow. The only trouble with him is he never got a right start in life. He would have turned out to be a good deal of a man if he had had the right kind of training."

The next day I met Jay and rather expected him to burst out against the Senator. His critique was condensed in about two sentences:

"Of course your friend Senator Brookhart is absolutely ignorant about European conditions, but he's a very decent fellow after all. The great trouble with the man is he got a wrong start in life, and never had any advantages."

But all things come to an end. Early one morning, approaching Vienna, we observed the lacelike spire of the beautiful Stephanskirche rising above the mists of the Danube Valley. We were on the last lap of our journey, having done a number of countries after leaving Rumania. I was in the position of an exhausted Channel swimmer, still beyond his depth, but with the shore in sight.

I invoked in Vienna the assistance of an old friend, Prentiss Terry, United States trade commissioner, who agreed to see the Senator around Vienna for a day, dine with him and listen to his discourse in the evening. Terry, scarcely turned thirty, was in the prime of life, eupeptic, red-blooded, ambitious, eager to please—in brief, a human dynamo. Along about ten o'clock at night, after a laborious day, he dropped in to see me at the Hotel Bristol. His dejected figure betokened a great change. He looked droopy, as if he had just risen from a sick bed. The poor fellow was obviously in the last stages of exhaustion.

"Doctor," he gasped, "I'm all in; I'm foundered. I'm only an ordinary human being; I'm not a caterpillar tractor!"

The next evening I was to say farewell to the Senator when his train pulled out for Paris from the West Station at ten o'clock. After a crowded day we discussed at dinner the success of the Rochdale system; and to guard against any possible failure to make the train, left the hotel at nine o'clock. Arriving at the station, we had more than a half-hour to wait, and occupied the time discussing the marvelous strides of the Austrians in cooperative endeavor. My heart was rather heavy at the thought of saying good-by to the Senator, but my feet were heavier still. I could barely drag myself about.

I inquired hopefully of a guard passing through the train, "This train leaves in about three minutes, *nicht wahr?*"

"You have plenty of time," he assured me. "The service has been interrupted and the train *bleibt* here until after midnight."

What must it be to feel like thirty at fifty? Never to experience emotions of fatigue or impatience? Travel does tax one's patience. The interruptions, the delays, the officiousness of officials, the apparent stupidities of foreigners, which, after all, are only a mirror of your stupidities in not better comprehending their language and habitudes. The broad-shouldered, clear-eyed Senator never suffers from fatigue, sleeplessness, headache, pyorrhea, the fall of dandruff or granulated eyelids. He tirelessly moves toward his objectives with the invincible obstinacy of an insect. He still has time to cultivate the esthetic faculty which is the beginning of all art. It's an instinct which many men cultivate late in life. Our great industrialists, dedicating their lives to steel or copper, retire at a mature age with their accumulated millions to collect Rembrandts and Botticellis. Along with the quickened sense of the beauty of life, they may acquire a taste for poetry.

In leading the filibuster against the Ship Subsidy Bill, on February 22, 1923, Mr. Brookhart remarked on the floor of the Senate, after speaking four hours:

"This is the natal day of George Washington, the Father of our country, the greatest filibusterer in history. It was George Washington who filibustered the American people clear out of the British Empire. And there were some compatriots of George Washington who did not like the looks of a tax on tea, and they filibustered that tea over into Boston Harbor. Yes, that occurred up in Boston—dear old Boston—

*"The home of the bean and the cod,*
*Where the Lowells speak only to Abbotts,*
*And the Abbotts speak only to God."*

At this juncture, the scholarly Senator Calder, of New York, interrupted with the suggestion that the Lowells speak to the Cabots rather than to the Abbotts.

Mr. Brookhart: "I accept the correction. I am not very strong on poetry anyhow."

Yes, the Senator is not strong on poetry; but

give him time. He has acquired a great many things which he didn't have when he first led the struggle between those who have not and those who have. He has acquired a nice home, though still mortgaged, with garden and trees, in one of the suburbs of Washington; drives a sturdy though not showy motor-car; his children are succeeding.

Some day he may become a bank president or a railroad director and wear a top hat and light-colored spats. But this is not a work of the imagination. Suffice it to say that most of the radicals in our American political history are prone to turn conservative. Cummings started life as a red-hot radical and later, softening into a conservative, was defeated by Brookhart. Such men as Senator Tillman and Senator Lenroot entered public life as militant radicals and later came to be classified as moss-grown conservatives. Colonel Bryan, who for twenty years castigated the money power, came to be rated as something of a moneyed man himself and died in his sleep after a comfortable dinner following a powerful speech defending the faith of the fathers. Senator Brookhart's ambition is to avoid turning conservative.

Human political institutions are not struck off out of hand. Organized society is not a contraption which one may tinker on as if it were a machine. The roots of what we are run far back into the past. Mr. Brookhart's European trip acquainted him with stabilities which rest on the experience of a thousand years, but also with the revolutions of the present day. As men come to know history—that is to say, the story of human experience on this planet—in brief, as they become educated they have to learn that the most successful peoples politically are not those of vain experiments who would make haste rapidly, but rather the slow-going, phlegmatic peoples, such as the British, the Dutch and the Swedes, who make haste slowly. When it comes to violent and extreme changes, the radicals and fanatics are really beaten before they start. They are up against the accumulated wills and experiences of the men who have gone before. What is this thing that wrings back every violent change in the social order and tends to restore the old balance? It is the thing which we call the past!

# What I Really Saw and Learned in Europe in 1923*

## IN CONTRAST WITH THE SCHOLARLY BUT PROVINCIAL PICTURE OF MY FRIEND AND TRAVELING COMPANION, DR. ALFRED PEARCE DENNIS

### By Smith Wildman Brookhart

EARLY in 1923 I planned a trip to Europe for two specific purposes—to bring the international rifle matches to the United States, if possible, and to investigate the growth and development of economic cooperation. My traveling companion was to have been Mr. Huston Thompson, chairman of the Federal Trade Commission, who also wanted to investigate the cooperatives. At the last moment the sickness of Mr. Thompson's father delayed his going, although he did go later, and his report on cooperation should be rated as one of the most valuable things yet done by the Federal Trade Commission.

Prior to starting, it was announced in the press that I would visit Europe to investigate coopera-

*From The Saturday Evening Post, March 12, 1930. Used by permission of the Author.

[ 62 ]

tion. President Hoover, then Secretary of Commerce, called me on the long-distance telephone from Washington, District of Columbia, at my home in Washington, Iowa, and asked to send with me his personal representative in Europe, Dr. Alfred P. Dennis, saying he desired accurate information about cooperation for himself and for his department. I welcomed this suggestion and it was arranged that Doctor Dennis should meet me at Cherbourg when I landed in France.

At New York I took the *President Monroe*, a government boat, since sold to private enterprise. On board, the first person I met was Christian Lynch, a steel manufacturer, a fine gentleman and an experienced traveler, from Harrisburg, Pennsylvania. He introduced me to Dr. George E. Raiguel, of Philadelphia, a noted lecturer, peace advocate and traveler. We had never met before, but soon became friends, and they both decided to change their route of travel and go with me. This they did, and stayed with me all around Europe. We went into port, but did not land, and I got a glimpse of Plymouth, England, from shipboard.

The first European I met was a Scotch captain of pilots, an ardent prohibitionist, and from the same town in Scotland as the ancestors of my predecessor, Senator Kenyon, with whom he was acquainted. We then crossed the Channel to Cherbourg, and Doctor Dennis appeared with his interpreter. You will note that he needed an interpreter. The real truth is that the worthy doctor's French was not much better than my own. In fact, in a test, the interpreter said I had the better pronunciation. I had read several books in the original French, including *Les Miserables*, and I get the news from a paper quite readily—likewise with German and Spanish—but I got little of this in school and, instead, dug it out for myself.

Doctor Dennis, like myself, was traveling light, and we at once decided we would not do much shining at banquets, dinners and dances, though we did eat wholesome and bountiful meals at farmhouses in many places.

I now had two doctors on my hands—both aristocrats from the scholarly but provincial East. Doctor Dennis was long a professor in Princeton University under Woodrow Wilson. He came with the learning, dignity and caution of his great school, modified by agreeable, versatile and energetic training in commercial salesmanship. Doctor Raiguel was a scientifically trained physician, who had quit his profession for the more inspiring pursuit of eloquence in social and political betterment and among the intellectually élite and fashionable.

Widely traveled, he had acquired a knowledge of almost every language, and was able to make known our wants in a ready-made and effective way under all circumstances. These two doctors were as different as moonlight and bright sunshine, but I liked them both, got much valuable assistance from both and still feel a deep friendship for both. However, I soon noticed an amusing and sometimes entertaining jealousy between them. For instance, Doctor Dennis in his article quotes me as using the expression "ain't you," and so on—an expression I never use except in derision. The only recollection of its use, in my mind, on the whole trip was when the doctor himself used it in reference to the other doctor, saying, "He knows more that ain't so than any man I ever met." Doctor Raiguel's retort was generous, admitting he was a "buttinsky" on the tour, and conceding the right of Doctor Dennis to criticize, and so I avoided all bloodshed.

We were ready for business, and I told Doctor Dennis I wanted to see the rifle associations, which would not take long, and then all my time would be given to the cooperatives. I had read the history of all the countries of Europe, ancient, medieval and modern. I had read and studied books of travel until I saw but few unfamiliar scenes on the whole tour. Therefore it was my plan to let the "dead past bury its dead," take a look at the living present, and raise, as far as possible, the curtain of the dawning future.

A study of cooperation had convinced me that it had grown into a great economic system. The war had augmented rather than retarded its growth. It was becoming a powerful competitor of the whole competitive system. Why should it not transact the business of the whole world? Why had it not succeeded so well in the United States? The latter question was conclusively answered at my first interview.

I wanted one minute at the tomb of Napoleon, a few more at the tomb of LaFayette, and a day on the battle-field of the World War, and then to my task. The commercial attachés were new to the government service, but they were enthusiastically efficient. Doctor Dennis was able to arrange our program in every country in advance, by the day and by the hour. It would have been humanly impossible to cover more ground or gather more reliable information in the same length of time.

My first interview was with Ambassador Herrick. My team had won his magnificent rifle trophies when he was governor of Ohio, but I had never met him. He was a gracious, a pleasing and a commanding personality. I told him my purpose was to investigate the cooperatives in the various countries of Europe. When I mentioned cooperatives his whole manner changed like magic. If he had shown such a thing as ambassadorial dignity, it disappeared in a flash. His whole being became earnestness and gravity. He dropped into his chair and said to me:

"Sit down! Sit down!" Then he said, "You are on the greatest mission in the world. The proudest heritage I have to claim is that my father successfully managed a cooperative store for twenty-four years."

I then knew he was a friend of cooperation, genuine, true, intelligent. He told me how Warren S. Stone had been a director in his great bank, The Society for Savings, at Cleveland, and how he had encouraged Stone to organize a genuine cooperative bank for the locomotive engineers. Then they were surprised to find that there was no law, either national or state, that would even permit the organization of a cooperative bank. I told him Stone was from my home town and that I had been with him in his labor convention when such a bank was planned.

Mr. Herrick then pushed a button, and a boy came in, and he directed this boy to bring a copy of his book on Rural Credits. In a few moments the boy was back. Mr. Herrick took the book, autographed it to me, and said—it lies on my desk as I write:

"I want you to read this book as you go around the countries of Europe, and you will find that the United States is the only civilized country in the world that by law prohibits the farmers or the laboring people from organizing their own savings in a cooperative banking system, with reserve bank, and all under their own control. Cooperation can never be a permanent success until it has such a system for its foundation."

For the first time I learned from the lips of this great man the true reason why cooperation had not succeeded better in the United States. And in his book, on page 479, he says:

There are no Federal or state laws in the United States under which the farmers might organize themselves into systems with credit societies as the basic units . . . . The farmers of the United States are capable and independent men, and they should have the right, under the laws, to organize themselves as best suits their own ideas or circumstances, whether in associations with shares or without shares, or with collective liability, limited or unlimited. Moreover, they should be able to decide for themselves whether they will have syndicated local associations or just one Raiffeisen credit society for each neighborhood. They have no choice under any of these laws, and thus the play of private initiative and the freedom of action is blocked.

Mr. Herrick told me how he had tried to get the American Bankers' Association to support a cooperative-banking law, but had failed; and we talked of a plan to get it indorsed by the Republican National Convention. A year later, when I was in Cleveland, he came in from his country home to see me, and we planned to have Senator Fess present his resolution to the resolutions committee; and that was done. This committee rejected the resolution.

Doctor Dennis, in his brilliant and scholarly account, sees nothing in all this but a freak of the western radical mind—and such is the eastern provincialism of scholarship. When I say "eastern provincialism," do not misunderstand me. The farmers of the East are not provincial. They are just like the farmers of the West—national in their view-point. The laborers of the East are also just like the laborers of the West. And now, the little business men, harassed and destroyed by chain-store monopolies, and the little bankers, threatened and closed up by the chain-bank autocracy, are talking with us about national cooperation. Even

the investors of the East, seeing their values destroyed by the speculative control of credit exactly
as the land values of the West have been destroyed,
are now taking a national look at cooperative banking. There are only the monopolies, the scholarship and the high society of the East that remain
provincial.

The day we landed at Cherbourg a great cooperative congress met at Bordeaux. The labor producers' cooperatives, the consumers' cooperatives
and the farmers' cooperatives were all federated
together into a great national unit. The center of
this was the cooperative banking system which had
been established since the war. We visited its reserve bank, already grown large; we visited many
cooperative stores and the great wholesale—much
the greatest in all France. The thing that impressed me most was the tremendous growth of it
all since the war. Other business had receded, but
cooperation had doubled, even trebled, in volume
of business, while its membership increased more
rapidly than in all its history. In the amusing article of Doctor Dennis you will find all of this to
be only a trivial Rochdale toy shop.

Our next move was to London. We visited the
head offices of the farmers' cooperatives but did
not find a great organization; however, its best

growth had been since the war. I was told that they had a committee in Denmark studying the Danish farmer cooperatives. Then I told them that, forty years before, Uncle Peder Pedersen, of Iowa, had been a member of a Danish committee of seven that came from Denmark to England to study Rochdale cooperation, and how they had learned it from English laboring people and had taken it back to the farmers of Denmark, where it had reached a stage of success equaled only by English labor; and now, forty years later, the farmers of Great Britain will bring it back to English agriculture.

We then went to Edinburgh, in Scotland, to the great congress of the Rochdale System. On the way, in several places, I saw the old English name Wildman, my own middle name, that I got from my mother, and with which I am always proud to warn all standpatters that I can not be tamed. This congress was composed of eighteen hundred delegates from Great Britain, and fraternal delegates from all other countries. I sat as a fraternal delegate from the Cooperative League of America. The English delegates represented more than six thousand cooperative stores, a cooperative wholesale at Newcastle as large as any private wholesale in the world, another at Glasgow, larger, and another at Manchester, three and one-half times as large as the one at Glasgow. These enterprises had a membership of four million five hundred thousand—mostly heads of families—thus representing more than a third of all the people of Great Britain. They were doing thirty per cent. of all the merchandising in England, Ireland, Scotland and Wales. They had one hundred fifty-eight large producing factories, including eleven great flour mills grinding thirty-five per cent. of all the flour used in Great Britain. They had their own coal mines, forty thousand acres of farms, the largest tea plantations in the world in the island of Ceylon, great wheat plantations in Canada, and some ships of their own. Their factories make nearly everything used in human civilization, and their business extends all around the world. They are the largest single buyer of wheat in either Canada or the United States. All this vast system rests upon the solid foundation of a cooperative banking system, with about six thousand little deposit banks—usually a department of a store—and a great reserve bank as a department of the wholesale; and this reserve bank alone had a turnover then of two billion five hundred million dollars and, in 1927, of more than three billion five hundred million dollars.

Before the war the total cooperative membership was about three million, in 1923 it was more than four million five hundred thousand, and in 1927 it was more than five million five hundred thousand. It has the best, most efficient, most scientific, most practical, most expert and most successful training school for managers of stores, banks and factories in the world. It is the big institution of Great Britain—and still, Doctor Dennis, in his article, walked all around it, over it, through it and under it, but never saw it except to recount my retort to the English lord who had never heard of it. It is growing six times as fast as the English population, and now has its first friendly government. It has had a like growth in Canada, Australia, South Africa, New Zealand and even India. It is inevitable that it will dominate the business of the English Empire in the near future.

All this was started by twenty-eight poor flannel weavers in 1844. It is built upon three basic principles—one man, one vote. Capital does not vote in the cooperative enterprise; men hire capital, and not capital hires men. Second, the earnings of capital are limited—five per cent. is all they pay, all capital ever expects, and they are the best-financed enterprises in Great Britain. Third, the trade dividend; twenty-five per cent. of the net is kept in the enterprise for absorption of losses, safety and growth. The balance of the net is distributed back to the members in proportion to the business transacted with the enterprise. Simple, yes, but this means the Sermon on the Mount, the Golden Rule in business. I can never forget the words of the secretary as he closed his report of these vast enterprises:

"Notwithstanding these millions and billions of money, there is not a millionaire amongst us. Co-operation never made a millionaire and it never made a pauper."

We visited the wholesales, the factories and the banks at Glasgow, Manchester and Newcastle-upon-Tyne. The week before we were in Glasgow the bank loaned the city five hundred thousand pounds, or two million five hundred thousand dollars, and it was financing twenty-seven big factories at the same time.

At Newcastle we took a Norwegian boat, the *Venus,* across the North Sea for Bergen, Norway. On the way we met the *Mercury,* the *Mars,* the *Jupiter* and all the rest of the solar system. We landed on a beautiful day and found the city in the hands of the communists. That did not alarm me or the rest of the party, but Doctor Dennis thought we ought to take the first train out, so off we started for Christiania—now Oslo—and were soon at the top of the mountains—the beautiful mountains of Norway. There we had our pictures taken in six feet of snow in June—not in July. It was here that the doctor's light coat came handiest to me, while his heavy underwear protected him. However, they were hardly needed, as the snow was melting and the girls were skipping around on skis with apparently no more clothes than they wear in Washington.

We found the same story of cooperative growth in Norway since the war, and especially among the farmers. Then we hastened to Stockholm, in Sweden. There we visited many cooperative enterprises and got the same story of greatly increased growth since the war. One of the most prized and pleasant incidents of the whole tour was a visit with Branting, the great Swedish statesman—since dead. Branting told me that cooperation was the great development and hope of his country, both for agriculture and industry, and said that it must rest upon cooperative banking.

Our next hop was to Denmark, to Copenhagen, the city of bicycles and the land of all kinds of cooperation. This little country is the delight of the farmers of the world. They learned cooperation in England, as I have said, under the leadership of my old friend, Uncle Peder Pedersen, the state organizer of the Iowa Farm Bureau Federation. In this country of Denmark they got ninety-five per cent. of the farmers into their cooperative organizations, and they are doing everything cooperatively, even controlling the government. We visited all their enterprises, from chicken hatchery to reserve bank, and found them all genuine Rochdale products.

The Danes have forty-six cooperative packing plants; the most efficient in the world except some in Ireland that are modeled after them. They call a half of a hog a piece of bacon, and they prepare it as father used to do in the old smokehouse. Their product in London was worth six cents a pound more than the best Tamworth from our great packing plants. There is no beef trust in Denmark. The dairy farms, the cheese factories and the creameries are a delight and a joy for ever. The only regret I have concerning Denmark is that Doctor Dennis put me in a picture out in front of a dairy cow, and labeled it "Inspecting a prize Danish bull." I must tell him something about zoology before he writes me up in another story. One thing about cooperation in Denmark was different from all other countries. It had not grown so much since the war. There was not so much room for growth. It was nearly all cooperative before the war.

Senator Brookhart, with overcoat, and author in Danish hog pen

Our next stop was in Germany. We had no visit that was busier or more profitable on the whole trip. Doctor Dennis has well described our activities, but again he played Hamlet, with Hamlet left out. The important thing we discovered was the enormous growth of cooperation since the war. The farm organizations had reached a membership of two million four hundred thousand—nearly half joining since the war. Labor had a membership of three million seven hundred fifty thousand—a tremendous increase since the war. The total membership was far greater than in Great Britain. They were well organized. The Germans have great power of organization. We visited their great cooperative banking systems—the Raiffeisen for the farmers, and the Schulze-Delitzsch for the consumers. We visited many enterprises—one of them the greatest bakery in the world. But they were in "hard lines," heavily pressed by the loss of the war, the occupation of the Rhineland and the Saar. The middle class was ruined by the depreciation of the mark. The first day in Berlin we bought fifty-seven thousand marks for a dollar. The last day we got eighty thousand. Even Doctor Cuno, the Chancellor, did not know where they would go. In the face of it all, they were determined to come back. They were loyal

[ 77 ]

to the new republic and done with Kaiserism and with war. If the burden of reparations is not too oppressive, I predict that this great and efficient people will speedily be molded into a cooperative republic and still win the war.

Poland was our next country, and Warsaw our next stop. Entering this reborn country, the emotions of any American will rise as he remembers the name of Kosciuszko and Pulaski. I also saw a park named Hoover, in appreciation of American relief after the World War. Witos, the farmer, was prime minister. The whole country was being organized cooperatively at a very rapid rate. The ablest man I saw was at the head of the cooperative banking system. I talked to the leading business men and bankers, and all said the cooperative method was the best way to do all business. I hope the dictatorship of Pilsudski has not destroyed this sentiment.

When in Berlin, I secured passports for myself, Doctor Raiguel and Mr. Lynch from the Russian Ambassador for a trip through Russia. I was unable to get permission for Doctor Dennis, because we had not recognized Russia and he was a government representative. There were many exceedingly interesting things in the Russian trip, but since Doctor Dennis could not go, I omit that from this article, except the briefest reference to cooperatives, and thus complete the chain of my story. At first the Soviet Government confiscated the cooperatives, but later decided to restore them. Lenin, in his last message to the Soviet Congress, made this recommendation. This is the only basic change they have made in their economic policy. Cooperation now has the hearty support of the government. I visited the big cooperative bank, stores and factories, and spent a day with the manager of the big wholesale—the same man who had managed it under the Czar. He told me his volume of business was six times what it had been before the revolution. So I found the greatest growth of all since the war was in Russia. It survived czarism, revolution, communism, pestilence and death. I can imagine no severer test of any economic idea. Before Doctor Dennis left us in Warsaw, he arranged with Admiral Bristol to send a destroyer from Constantinople to pick us up at Odessa. Accordingly we were met by Captain Field, with the destroyer *Goff*, and stayed over an extra day at Odessa. No feature of the tour was more delightful than the Black Sea cruise to Constantinople.

There was much of great interest in Constantinople, but not in reference to cooperation; so I pass it by. There was a revolution in Bulgaria, and Admiral Bristol thought best to send us past that country in the destroyer to Constantza, in Rumania, where we bade good-by to Captain Field and his delightful crew. We took a train to Bucharest and there rejoined Doctor Dennis, a day late. He was greatly perturbed and thought the Bolsheviks had impounded us, because he did not know of our day at Odessa, and no word came to him from Constantinople because of the Bulgarian revolution.

Rumania was filled with deepest interest, and cooperation had grown—but I must hasten. Minister Jay asked me interminable questions about Russia, but I enjoyed them all, as well as his fine dinner. I really think I was more comfortable in my travel-stained clothes than was the Minister in his soup-and-fish outfit.

We still had to make middle Europe. Hungary added but little to our information, but Czecho-Slovakia was a great delight, and told us as much as Denmark. It is a cooperative country now. They were changing the sugar refineries into farmers' cooperatives at that time. Their cooperative banking system and all their organizations were as good as the English, but were agricultural rather than industrial. The government was supporting the cooperative movement in every detail. The President was absent on a health vacation, but one of my most profitable visits was with Benes, the distinguished Minister of Foreign Affairs.

Vienna was the next stop, and the cooperative congress was in session. I talked with the leaders of all parties, and all agreed cooperation was the only hope of Austria.

I was next off at Zurich, in Switzerland—most beautiful Switzerland, cooperative Switzerland, rifle-shooting Switzerland, the home of the distant ancestors of my father. The return was then back through France and up through "Flanders fields where poppies grow." La Belle France! I did not find France decadent, but as virile as any country in Europe. There were things I did not approve, but they must not be charged to a whole people.

Belgium told me the same story of cooperative growth, and I passed over to Ireland, where Sir Horace Plunkett had made fifty speeches before he succeeded in organizing the first cooperative creamery. But I found cooperation a growing success in Ireland now, and spent a day at Plunkett House with "Æ," the poet, painter, cooperator and fellow laborer with Sir Horace.

The last stop was at Manchester, the financial and economic center of cooperation in the world. As Mr. Thorpe, the great manager, pointed out to me the world-wide scope, the irresistible growth,

the undeniable soundness, the Golden Rule spirit
and the universal benefits, it seemed to me one must
roll Henry Ford, Elbert H. Gary and Pierpont Morgan into one to make a Thorpe for efficiency alone.
Above all, this vast cooperative business is under
absolutely democratic control.

I was ready to come home, yes, but I had stopped
to see Ambassador Herrick again. He was eager
for every word about Russia, and ready for recognition. He urged me to call on the foreign offices
in both France and England. He arranged for me
to meet Poincaré, but I had gone to Château-
Thierry before the information reached me, and I
talked to his under-secretary instead. I told them
the story as I saw it, and it was welcomed at the
French office, but not so in England or by Secretary Hughes at home.

At odd times I had talked to Doctor Dennis
about economic questions like transportation,
credit control, agricultural equality, the earnings
of the whole people and the laws affecting their
distribution. I talked in details and exact facts,
of which I have made an exact record in many discussions and investigations, but in his brilliant
article they all slide off his polished mind like
water off a duck. The most complete set of facts
impressed him only as "fetishes." I worked out

the railroad facts with Senator Cummins, and we agreed for fifteen years. The only reason I could defeat him was because they were facts and I stuck to them. The facts that I gave Doctor Dennis about the deflation of the farmers by the Federal Reserve Board were taken from the Manufacturers' Record, the exact minutes of the Board itself, letters from the Reserve banks, a detailed study of the markets, and a wide technical study of the whole banking question, including books published by the Reserve banks. Most of the facts I have discussed with members of the Federal Reserve Board, and not one that I use is even disputed.

Notwithstanding all this, the only impression that Doctor Dennis mentioned was that "In the summer of 1920 two Wall Street magnates were strolling up Broadway. One turned to the other and remarked, 'Well, I guess it's about time we deflate the farmer.'" After all the pains I took with Doctor Dennis, a mythical result like this is discouraging, to say the least. However, I am both patient and persistent, and I still have hope. I have always known that a proposition must be stated at least three times to be clearly understood by the ordinary mind. I still think six times will take it home to the college mind and, I hope, to the whole of eastern provincial scholarship.

# CHAPTER III

## WOODROW WILSON, PRINCETON SCHOOLMASTER

LOOKING back through the thickening mists of thirty-five years, I see the vivid apparition of Professor Wilson in his Princeton classroom. Dickinson Hall, where he lectured, has been razed these many years to give ground for a splendid new academic building. The material self of Professor Wilson also has fallen, but no splendid successor has risen to occupy his vacant place.

I write of him out of my own vivid memories of his personality and of his teachings. As to his public career and the great transactions in which he bore a part, I can write no better, and probably no worse, than some millions of his contemporaries. I shall stick to what I know of him from personal contacts corresponding to a period in his life about which relatively little has been recorded. The record of his schoolmaster days is to be read in the intangible influence of his teachings upon the minds and hearts of his students.

What I am trying to present is a picturization of a tiny segment of the great sphere of a great man's life. I knew him well during the first four years

of his teaching work at Princeton. Not being satisfied with two elective courses under him in my
senior year, I returned for three years of postgraduate work, taking every course which Professor Wilson offered during his teaching days at
Princeton.

Professor Wilson came to Princeton from Wesleyan University in the autumn of 1890 to fill the
chair of jurisprudence and political economy. As
a young Titan in the educational world, he made a
great stir from the start. His political writings—
notably *Congressional Government* and *The State*,
the one a masterful dissection of our public-law
system, the other a review of the morphology of
our own state system and those of Europe—brought
him wide public recognition. What was more important to the undergraduates was his fame as a
patron of athletics. His title deeds to glory in this
respect turned out to be defective. He was never
on the personal side a devotee of athletics, and his
interest in football, the major Princeton sport, was
like the seed which sprang up apace on stony
ground but withered quickly for lack of root. In
the year preceding Mr. Wilson's avatar, Princeton's
star team of veterans had overwhelmed both ancient rivals—Yale and Harvard. In the following
season the situation was completely reversed. Most

of the crack players had been lost through graduation, and the first and only Princeton team which Professor Wilson coached on the field was a lamentably weak one and was beaten by Yale at the close of the season by the heart-breaking score of 32 to 0. My classmate, Edgar Poe, of the famous Baltimore football family of Poes, captained the team in both years. He says of Professor Wilson's coaching that it was inspiring but not instructive.

But as I say, his fame as a patron of athletics at Wesleyan had preceded him. The tale ran that, smarting under the injustice of a rank decision against Wesleyan in a football game with Amherst, Professor Wilson had rushed on to the field demanding the immediate expulsion of an obviously incompetent referee—indeed, some had it that he cried out, "Kill the referee!" This, of course, is one of those myths that great enthusiasms weave about heroic personalities. It is enough to say that Professor Wilson came to us with the happiest credentials. We expected great things of him, and our hopes were not disappointed when we gathered in Dickinson Hall for the first lecture of his first course.

How Mr. Wilson came to consider himself unprepossessing in appearance, I can't imagine. His first appearance made quite the contrary impression on us. At the age of thirty-four, he was a man you would turn twice to look at in a crowd, and he became more distinguished and patrician-looking as he grew older. He knew the arts of pleasing—particularly mass pleasing. I should rather have looked like Wilson than any matinée idol of his generation. His lean spareness of figure conveyed the impression of dominating height as he stood on the lecture platform, an impression which was lost, of course, with later-day accretions of flesh. His prognathous Hapsburg jaw closed after a rounded period with the snap of finality. Every inch of the jaw—and there were three inches of it—was that of fighting man and oracle combined. Those windows of the soul, his luminous eyes, looking out of the body, commanded it, but these same eyes, reflected backward to the seat of intelligence, indeed conveyed the impression of pure intelligence itself. His mind worked as if he secreted thought easily, naturally, unaffectedly, as a cow secretes milk or the liver secretes bile.

His teeth were lamentably bad, ignobly patched and cobbled by sundry artificers in metals. The consummate arts of odontology in later years completely redressed to outward seeming these defects of Nature. His smile thus became more engaging

[ 87 ]

with the years. His black stringy locks, which later became a beautiful silver, revealed his character—hair typical of the man, stark, straight and unsocial, rather than sleek, sinuous and gregarious. He waxed in personal pulchritude with the passing years. He was never so handsome as the day he was driven through the streets of Rome in a landau, seated beside the abbreviated King of Italy. It was the American rather than the Roman who looked the part of Imperial Cæsar returning from successful wars.

He dressed, as some erroneously thought, after the fashion of a southern gentleman, appearing before us in a black cutaway coat, low turnover collar with black string tie, looking quite the part of a non-conformist Scotch parson or a meticulous undertaker's assistant officiating at an ambitious shabby-genteel funeral. His spike-tail coat served when he mounted a bicycle as well as on the lecture platform. His home on Library Place was a goodish mile from his lecture room and he found a time conservator in his bicycle, which he bestrode with the stately dignity of the King of Siam making stately progress on the back of the royal white elephant. The low collar disclosed beneath an Adam's apple, which oscillated as he talked, a wisp of nethermost beard which through its strategic defensive situation remained unscathed by the ravages of an inimical razor.

Professor Wilson habitually stood during his lectures. Speaking from a mere skeleton of notes, he hammered in his teachings with an up-and-down, full-armed gesture. Thus he was a perpendicular lecturer, his talking nose and his oscillating Adam's apple moving up and down with speech, along with his pump-handle gestures. He gestured as if operating the handle of a spray pump. He was there to spray students with a shower of knowledge, his superior mind acting downward upon the mass—a Scotch Covenanter bent upon describing how man acts politically, hammering information into reluctant minds. He was essentially the lecturer rather than the teacher, nor were his lectures as helpful as the books, such as Bagehot and Dicey, from which his own inspirations were drawn. Having sprayed his audience, Professor Wilson little recked whether inoculations of knowledge took or not. In those days not a few indolent, good-natured students attended lectures as a matter of condescending concession to certain disagreeable academic formalities.

These lollers out front conveyed the tacit challenge: "Here we are. Teach us something if you can!" Unimpressionable Arctic puffin birds of the classroom! But as far as Professor Wilson was concerned, the loafers could either take it or leave it. He gaged his discourse to the requirements of the serious-minded, taking no pains to conceal his contempt for inferior minds. Unlike the Great Apostle who suffered fools gladly, Professor Wilson suffered them not at all.

Professor Wilson could not bear to be crossed and his dignity was quick to resent restlessness, inattention or the least sign of disorder in his classroom. He conducted his classes with an air of imperiousness, suggesting the grand manner just as his writings carry the suggestion of the grand style. He clearly imitated Burke—a master in the use of the grand style. A whispered conversation in the back benches would instantly stiffen him into the grim, magisterial defender of his own dignity. His stock rebuke, uttered with Olympian superiority, was: "Gentlemen, try to remember that you are supposed to be gentlemen."

Professor Wilson's touchiness, his quick irritation over trifles, may be laid, I think, in some measure to the fact that he was unused to opposition at home. Mrs. Wilson was put into this world, it would seem, to make it an easy place to live in for those she loved. His three daughters also lived to please and to ease. Professor Wilson,

Professor Wilson hurrying to his classes—year 1891

habituated at home to ease, to softness, to amiable compliances, never got to understand how people can be rude, thoughtless, uncomprehending, non-cooperative. If he had been blessed with a head-strong if not troublesome son, he would have better known how to be patient under the irritations of jarring, difficult, cantankerous souls.

In his younger and obscure days, I am wondering if he ever consciously put before himself an exalted self which he intended to realize. He could say, "These are my books, this is my typewriter, this is my gifted brain—what are these things for?" And he could answer, "They are for me—for my help, my convenience, my security, my livelihood." But did he ever ask himself, "These things being for me, what am I for?" What was his *summum bonum*? Fame? Glory? Yes, he intensely craved honor, esteem, fame. These things he set about to attain, hitching together a powerful thinking machine with habits of invincible industry. He was as industrious as Mr. Hoover, without possessing Mr. Hoover's genius for the concrete. He was as zealous in answering the great call as Peter the Hermit or Paul the Apostle, but they sought after an incorruptible crown.

He cared little for the affection or companionship of men. He never could have been a clubman or risen to phantom dignity as a Serene Potentate in a fraternal lodge. In the classroom he was theorist rather than idealist. He had no concrete proposals to make for augmenting human happiness—indeed, he ignored the element of individual happiness—but he had principles to apply, and these principles, though agreeable to the auditory nerve, were on analysis difficult of practical application. Later the world came to know of him through the enunciation of felicitous phrases which were flattering to the human heart but contradictory to the human understanding: "Making the world safe for democracy"; "Open covenants openly arrived at"; "The heart of the world is awake and the heart of the world needs to be satisfied"; "Self-determination" for the divers swarming peoples that dwell upon the surface of this planet.

Professor Wilson could always find in convenient doctrines a refuge from inconvenient facts. He had a striking talent too for definitions which inadequately defined a subject by over-defining it. He stated on one occasion that his father had taught him the value of definitions. Here is how he defined the properties of political sovereignty: 1. Habit of obedience; 2. Sentiment of loyalty; 3. Reverence; 4. Sense of duty; 5. Fear or awe; 6. Race or national feeling. One might, of course, add a half-dozen more attributes, just as one might analyze Lincoln's Gettysburg Address by breaking it down into its attributes: 1. Simplicity; 2. Sincerity; 3. Earnestness; 4. Tenderness; 5. Clarity; 6. Restraint; 7. Propriety; 8. Precision; 9. Purity; 10. Solemnity; etc., but after all the attributes have been catalogued, the best estimate of the qualities of the address is the thing itself. He defines the Federal State as composed of "self-originated, self-constituted, self-competent, self-sustaining, veritable communities." Almost any intelligent man with a feeling for the concrete would find something lacking in this definition. The concept of sovereignty, by the way, was one of his pet topics for discussion. He would comment by the hour upon the conflicting notions of such publicists as John Austin and Sir Henry Maine and delighted to follow Dicey in the contrast he draws between the American types of non-sovereign law-making bodies and the legislative omnipotence of the British Parliament. So far so good; it was delightful; but the moment he began to turn aside to his own abstractions, as for example to the discovery of the locus of sovereignty in the United States, he would wind up with the academic conclusion that the locus of sovereign power in our governmental system is to be found in a duly organized, constitutional convention clothed with power to modify our existing organic law. The plain man with a feeling for the concrete would not have to go so far as a hypothetical constitutional convention. He would find the locus of sovereignty in the policemen's club, the tax collector's bill, the sheriff's writ. The practical man sees sovereignty diffused through a multitude of local, state and federal organs of authority, with supreme power ultimately lodged in the living, breathing millions of persons who compose the citizenry of this Republic.

Professor Wilson was wont to insist that sovereignty was not susceptible of limitation. That is the juridical view. Blackstone undoubtedly would agree, but Blackstone was concerned with the letter, with the written word. *Littera scripta manet*. But the letter killeth. If you go by the written word, you have an entirely false idea of both the British Constitution and our own. Of course, to the practical man sovereignty is susceptible of limitation, if by nothing else by the community's habit of obedience, by revolution, by assassination. Walter Bagehot more than any other master was Professor Wilson's guide and pattern. The Wilsonian style as well as its content of doctrine was formed by Bagehot, Burke, Maine, Dicey, but Bagehot is king of them all. Bagehot too was given to definition, though his definitions are not a string of attributes but epigrams as sound as they are colorful and clever. For example, Bagehot defines a constitutional statesman as a "man of common opinions and uncommon abilities." He distinguishes between a civilized man and a savage by pointing out that a savage is unable to postpone the present to the future. He describes the emptiness of the voluptuary's life as misery striving to be gay and gaiety feeling itself to be miserable. If for nothing else, I have to be thankful to Professor Wilson for introducing me to Bagehot and Burke, but particularly to Bagehot whose style and savor so got hold of me that to this day I risk unconscious plagiarism of Bagehot in everything I attempt to write.

Professor Wilson, like other scholars with a taste for history, was strong on the genetics of the state. He would theorize both backward and forward, taking us backward to the uttermost limbo of the known facts of human group life on this planet and beyond that into the fields of pure speculation or, again, on an ascending scale, he would carry his speculations about the state into the rarefied air of German metaphysics. He recoiled before the concrete. As far as I can recall, he made no

mention in his course—Administration—of the
Interstate Commerce Commission. For some years
the writer has been a member of one of the federal
administrative boards—the United States Tariff
Commission—but Professor Wilson's course in Administration did not supply what the scientific
man would call a chemical trace of practical
preparation for his daily task as a petty governmental administrator. That might not have been
Professor Wilson's fault, since a lecturer may give
a dull student information without giving him understanding. So one might say that he had never
been able to make the smallest practical use of
higher mathematics studied in college. We received, however, from Professor Wilson things that
are more valuable than practical profit. He had
an affection for certain words, and one of his
blessed and overworked words was "fountain."
He himself was a fountain—a fountain of inspiration. The best thing which many of us received from Princeton was not information but
inspiration.

So it was that Professor Wilson opened the doors
of an ampler life to us. As for what he actually
taught, it was the inspiration of his personality
rather than what he actually taught that caused
our hearts to burn within us while he talked with

us by the way. His was precisely the type of scholarship which would have won me to the man. Forty years ago this country was swept by a craze for the German type of dry-as-dust scholarship. It was about the time that kiln-dried historical students were toppling Macaulay from his pedestal and enthroning the dreary and meticulous Stubbs in his stead. Let us be thankful that, according to the precepts of the day Professor Wilson did not undertake an analysis of the functions of the Carlovingian Mayors of the Palace or delve into the genealogies of the Hittite kings.

An anatomist seeking to know the secrets of the human body dissects a cadaver with the breath barely out of its body; he is not asking to work with fossil bones unearthed in the Gobi Desert. *Non omnia possumus omnes.* We can't all be Leonardo da Vincis. Plodding scholars we must have, just as there must be cart horses as well as race horses. The most scholarly student I knew in Princeton was a man of the plodding type who led our class consistently for four years. His studies in English literature led him back to the old texts of Bede and Cædmon, and these in turn to the parent Germanic languages, and these again into the far hinterlands of Sanskrit and whatever might lie beyond. A revered scholar who could parse in Icelandic and

pun in Coptic, for all I know. He came as near
as any living man to settling the vexed question,
raised in the Vedas, as to whether the implements
used in braying shoots of the haoma in the pre-
Indian ethnic period were press stones such as
mortar and pestle or a press of the type described
by Apastamba, representing a crude form of re-
volving millstones.

> He settled *Hoti's* business—let it be!—
> Properly based *Oun*—
> Gave us the doctrine of the enclitic *De*,
> Dead from the waist down.

The subject of his doctor's thesis was The Gruhasangraha—Parisishta of Gobilaputra. Such scholarship does great honor to a man, but it is not for
the multitude.

The powerful mind of Professor Wilson trans-
muted baser elements into golden inspirations, and
made his culture accessible to the multitude above
whom he towered. There is nothing ignoble in
knowledge, even though it be useless. Art is long
and time is fleeting, with most of us under the necessity of sweating for our daily bread and butter.
Culture is a long job.

Professor Wilson was not born to be a Grad-
grind scholar; he was essentially a man of humane
letters, and that was the self that he consciously

set before himself to be realized. He spoke to be heard; he wrote to be read. He schooled himself in the arts of persuasion. His scholarly passion was not horizontal, pushing to the far periphery of the known in seeking to lift the veil which divides it from the infinite spaces of the unknown. His passion was vertical; he would tread the dominating heights. This passion for dominion goaded him to the end—hastened the end.

"You may write a chronicle," he tells us, "but you will not serve yourself thereby. You will only serve some fellow who will come after you, possessing what you did not have—an ear for the words you could not hit upon; an eye for the colors you could not see; a hand for the strokes you missed."

Let the pedant retailers of dulness attend to the coral-insect business, each man furnishing his mite to the great reef of human knowledge. Dull boys who know everything about literature except how to write it or how to enjoy it. Professor Wilson taught himself the artistry of writing. The cultivation of the language one speaks is the most important factor, I take it, in a liberal education.

Professor Wilson's genius for the spoken and written word was a genius that consisted in infinite capacity for taking pains. He labored for a dis-

tumble of college life, from all the contacts of every sort and condition of men, and you have done a thing which America will brand with its contemptuous disapproval."

Any one of twenty criticisms might have been made against Professor West's graduate-school program. Professor Wilson chose to fight the project on the democratic issue.

Years after, Professor Wilson, as President of the United States, delivering a memorial address at the door of the lowly backwoods cabin where Abraham Lincoln was born had this to say:

"How eloquent this little house. Within this shrine is of the vigor of democracy. There is nowhere in the land any home so remote, so humble, that it may not contain the power of mind and conscience to which nations yield and history submits its processes. Genius is no snob; it affects humble company as well as great; it serenely chooses its comrade. This little hut was the cradle of one of the great sons of men who presently emerged upon the great stage, himself the center of the great plot. It demonstrates the vigor of democracy. Such are the authentic proofs of the validity and vitality of democracy. Here no less hides the mystery of democracy. Who shall guess this secret of nature and providence and a free polity?"

Do we account for the great-souled Lincoln in these mystic phrases about democracy? What was the relation of causality between Lincoln's genius and democracy? Possibly Lincoln might have been a mute, inglorious Milton but for the opportunities afforded by democracy. Certainly a man stands a better chance of making something of himself when born into the wide opportunities of America than into the narrow opportunities of China; yet democracy has little to do with the manifestations of human genius in the world. The great efflorescence of many-sided geniuses of the Italian Renaissance corresponded precisely with the age of despots in Italian history. Michael Angelo owed nothing to democracy but much to the patronage of the Papal Court. What is the connection between Mussolini's powerful personality and democracy? Long before democracy was recognized as a workable theory of government for great nations obscure and lowly men came to sit in the chair of Saint Peter, the highest position to which the sons of men might aspire. Jesus of Nazareth, the humble provincial, founder of a despised sect of an outcast race was born in a stable.

Professor Wilson possessed a positive genius for covering an entire plexus of ideas with some suavely elegant moral doctrine. He believed in democracy in much the way the Russian leaders of to-day subscribe to the doctrines of communism. We render lip service to some beautiful doctrine of non-resistance, but it's something to declaim by and not something to live by. Men with a gift of eloquence, speaking down to the masses from a platform, are under a constant temptation to tell the audience what the orator thinks it would like to hear rather than attempt to lift the audience to the level of his own sincerities. It is hard not to take short-cuts to appreciation, such as palpable hits, unqualified generalizations, crudifications rather than clarifications of the issue. When all else fails to stir a popular audience, let the band strike up *Dixie*.

Students are not the best judges or the most lenient critics of the young professor during the trying years he is organizing his material. After taking three courses under Professor Wilson, my interest began to wane. Even professors themselves tire of their own repetitions, and their task would become intolerable if they were not inspired by the eager interest of new classes, to whom the old story is a fresh revelation. And so it was that, after four years of Professor Wilson's lectures, I came to tire of definitions and repetitions, unrealities. One began to question his infallibility—particularly his judicial instinct. His temper was easily irritated by dissent, nor could he brook any rival in his field. Prof. William M. Sloane, head of the history department, lectured to crowded classrooms. A latent antagonism developed between the two men, with bad feeling displayed on both sides in later years.

I had taken all of Professor Sloane's courses and had been awarded, on his recommendation, fellowships for two succeeding years. In the winter of 1893, Professor Sloane was granted leave of absence and sailed for Europe. He commissioned me to examine the papers submitted in competition for two history prizes to be awarded the following commencement. In making the awards, I found difficulties in choice as between two papers of somewhat equal merit. I applied to Professor Wilson for help. He graciously received me in his home on Library Place, one May afternoon, and made no difficulty about complying with my request. Warmly suffused with pleasure over my charming reception, I made my adieus and had reached the front door when Professor Wilson called me sharply back; his voice was cold and incisive:

"I see these papers are submitted in competition for the Class of 1876 history prize. Why did you not tell me you were asking me to do Sloane's work for him?"

"I was asking a favor for myself and not for Professor Sloane, who knows nothing about it," I replied.

With his square jaw set high, he brushed aside the explanation:

"Professor Sloane is enjoying himself in Europe; I am swamped with work here. I am something of a logician—either Professor Sloane should remain at home and attend to his own business or else leave some one in his stead capable of doing so."

I started to speak and, indeed, did form sentences, but my words were as ineffectual as the buzz of a gnat above the roar of Niagara. Without another word, he handed me the two offending papers and dismissed me by turning to his typing machine.

Try as I might, I could never get back into his good graces. I had done an unpardonable thing. Attempts to soften his heart had about the same effect as a lighted parlor match on the polar ice cap.

As Cibber is reported to have remarked of the great Doctor Johnson: "There is no use arguing with him, for when his pistol misses fire, he knocks you down with the butt end of it."

In the case of Professor Wilson, the man who disagreed with him was often not worth taking a

Dear Mr. Dennis,

Will you not be kind enough to say, in the "Here and There" of the Princetonian that I was unable to meet my classes this week on account of sickness?

I have been suffering in a way that made me feel very much more like de-composition than composition.

Very truly Yours,
Woodrow Wilson

Mr. A. P. Dennis

Characteristic note written by Professor Wilson to the author in 1891.
To the end he found amusement in a play of words and in limericks

pistol to; instead, he consigned you to an oubliette.

When Doctor Patton unexpectedly resigned the presidency of Princeton, he suggested Professor Wilson to the trustees as his successor. In his brilliant inaugural address, the new president had much to say about Princeton, past, present and future, but not a word about his predecessor, Doctor Patton.

Later, when Doctor Patton was made president of Princeton Theological Seminary, President Wilson was asked to deliver an address. It was a finished effort in every respect except that it made no reference directly or indirectly to Doctor Patton. It was clear that Professor Wilson did not approve of Doctor Patton.

Early disciples, such as myself, followed Professor Wilson's rise to fame with pride and exultation, but of necessity we followed him afar off. What seemed at first but a frail and impalpable barrier—his displeasure over some small matter—really proved to be a wall of adamant against which one might beat out one's life in vain.

"We that had loved him so, followed him, honoured him,
    Lived in his mild and magnificent eye,
Learned his great language, caught his clear accents,
    Made him our pattern to live and to die!"

[ 111 ]

On all the duties, rights, proprieties and obligations of life, Professor Wilson had his unalterable code. He interpreted non-conformity as a species of treason. The essence of treason is giving aid and comfort to the enemy. His brain rather than his heart governed him in estimates of human conduct.

Deficient in sympathy himself, he was hurt and worn down in the end by the inevitable misunderstandings, frustrations and unfairness of minds that possessed the same unyielding, non-cooperative qualities as his own.

If he had possessed the heart of a Lincoln, history, with clear and luminous eyes, might have seen in him another Lincoln; but his speech proceeded from the head rather than the heart.

Will the suave and measured cadences of any speech of Mr. Wilson live with Lincoln's Gettysburg speech? Will any polished letter of Mr. Wilson survive Lincoln's note to Mrs. Bixby?

Here is the Lincoln letter written from the heart to Mrs. Bixby some sixty-six years ago:

[November 21, 1864.]

"Dear Madam:

"I have been shown in the files of the War Department a statement of the Adjutant-General of Massachusetts that you are the mother of five sons who have died gloriously on the field of battle. I feel how weak and fruitless must be any word of mine which should attempt to beguile you from the grief of a loss so overwhelming. But I cannot refrain from tendering to you the consolation that may be found in the thanks of the republic they died to save. I pray that our Heavenly Father may assuage the anguish of your bereavement, and leave you only the cherished memory of the loved and lost, and the solemn pride that must be yours to have laid so costly a sacrifice upon the altar of freedom.

"Yours very sincerely and respectfully,
"ABRAHAM LINCOLN."

If President Wilson had been moved under similar circumstances to write to Mrs. Bixby, it is not improbable that the letter would have read somewhat as follows:

"Dear Madam:

"I have learned through the duly constituted military authorities that your five noble-hearted sons have given their lives to America. May I not embrace this opportunity to observe that America took its origins in visions of free and common counsel? Your valiant sons died to hold the counsels of America together. If I did not believe that, I should not believe in democracy. If I did not believe that, I would not believe that people are fit to govern themselves. If I know the temper of America to-day, and I am fain to believe that I do know America's temper—America is quick with the purposes and processes of democracy. Your sons, if I do not mistake the breed, are of the stuff of that noble fighting stock who would be quit of tyranny and who with united counsel set up this government of America. Valor is no snob. It affects humble company as well as great. It serenely chooses its comrades. And here, if I see clear, lies the authentic proofs of the vigor and validity of democracy. Here no less lies the mystery of democracy. Who shall guess this secret of nature and providence and a free polity? It is our lofty privilege and our solemn duty to consecrate ourselves afresh to these high objects for which your sons nobly fought and died.

"Cordially yours,
"WOODROW WILSON."

After leaving Princeton, a great interval of time and space lay between the writer and President Wilson. Years later, he burst dazzlingly upon us in Italy as the apparition of a superman. I was serving in the American Embassy in Rome as commercial attaché.

President Wilson's welcome surpassed in fervor and magnitude anything that might be imagined. Imperial Cæsar returning in triumph from the wars never received a more delirious acclaim by Roman citizens. To the Italians, he was more than a personality—he was a symbol of deliverance.

Poverty-stricken and oppressed human beings viewed him through the haze of faith, yearning, ignorance. The old Italian charters of emancipation were palimpsests scrawled over with defeated hopes and unfulfilled desires. President Wilson, the savior, was a blank scroll upon which every man inscribed his dreams and his aspirations.

George Creel, able advertiser, had distributed poster pictures of the American President by the million. Candles burned in humble huts before the paper likeness of the American President, and simple-minded peasants knelt before these simulacra of the Great Deliverer, half in admiration, half in interrogation.

Then came the swift reverse! The hopes of the Italians were dashed in pieces; the nation was frustrated and confounded by a single will. President Wilson awarded the Adriatic port of Fiume, claimed by the Italians, to the Jugo-Slavs. Orlando returned from Paris as a protest against the Wilson verdict.

The tide of anger and bitterness rose to such a point that it became necessary for the American

Embassy in Rome to be protected from mob violence by a platoon of Italian soldiers.

During the customary recriminations with an Italian hack driver over the amount of his tip, Italian words were spoken which can bear no repetition here. But the crowning imprecation and ultimate insult lay in the phrase:

*"Sei figlio di Veelson!"* (Thou art a son of Wilson!)

Yes, I was a son of Wilson, and proud of it. Wilson had helped to form me back in those university days in Princeton. In that narrow life of a small world, he had been an inspiring influence. Now, in the great life of the huge world, he had become a mighty influence. He who had taught the principles of political sovereignty in the fetid atmosphere of a Dickinson Hall classroom had now become sovereign lawgiver in his own right for the world.

Some years later, for the last time, I was brought within physical nearness to my old Princeton professor. Mr. Hoover had called me back to Washington to serve him, and I was living within a few blocks of Mr. Wilson's home on S Street. For days he lay dying, with weeping men and women on their knees, silently praying, in the hushed street.

"Alas, alas," cried the dying pagan warrior, "what is this thing stronger than the strength of kings that pulls down the mightiest of warriors!"

Is there a further chapter in the amazing career of the man? What lies behind the mysterious veil that shrouds the state of the dead from that of the living? What of permanency in this shadowy world stretching out into thousands of years will survive his transient earthly endeavors? What will ultimately be salvaged from the wreck that is the doom of all human deeds? One wonders.

"There are no fields of amaranth on this side the grave; there are no voices, O Rhodope, that are not soon mute, however tuneful; there is no name, with whatever emphasis of passionate love re-peated, of which the echo is not faint at last. . . ."

# CHAPTER IV

## CALVIN COOLIDGE—AFTER TWENTY-FIVE YEARS

CONSIDERING the brevity of human life, twenty-five years is quite an interval, whether measured in time or experience. One's endowment-insurance policy falls due at the end of twenty years. Somehow when the policy is written, one is a bit dubious whether one will live to reap its benefits in person. When I first knew Calvin Coolidge he was always doing the unexpected thing or attaining his little end unaccountably. He puzzled me. To-day, after twenty-five years, he seems as clear and as natural to me as sunshine or limpid water.

I can write nothing new of Mr. Coolidge except in terms of my own knowledge of him. A great many people have written about him. I can only try to write of him rather than about him. I have nothing to give except in terms of my own experience. We both started work in Northampton, Massachusetts, in the late 'nineties, he a fledgling lawyer just out of Amherst, I a professor in Smith College with a few Princeton degrees as an evidence of good faith. We lodged almost within a stone's throw of each other, took our meals together in an unpretentious little hotel on a side-street called Rahar's Inn. Fought each other tooth and nail politically, respected each other and occasionally groped around for each other's companionship.

This was all twenty-five years ago, and as to his larger life in the ampler world of state and national politics I have no special knowledge and nothing whatever to contribute. One runs the risk of seeming egotistical, but there is no help for it when it comes to weighing another's personality in terms of one's own experience. From the first he piqued my interest, his arid personality, the puzzle that he should get on in life when logically he ought to stick fast, imprisoned in the narrow shell of his own limitations. I began by underestimating him and kept on doing so until I had been soundly punished for my errors of opinion, correction being administered by Mr. Coolidge himself.

Coolidge shared modest quarters on Round Hill with Rob Weir, steward of the Clark School. I lodged a little more pretentiously in a mansion at the foot of Round Hill. We frequently fell into step as we started down-town in the morning for the day's work. I have a perfect picture of young Coolidge as he strode down Elm Street some twenty-five years ago. Not a magnetic personality.

Had he been simply mediocre and commonplace, one would have gained no clearer impression of him at all. But just as a man may be so picturesquely ugly as to attract attention, so Coolidge's personality was apparently so negative that it at once challenged human interest. In appearance he was splendidly null, apparently deficient in red corpuscles, with a peaked, wire-drawn expression. You felt that he was always about to turn up his coat collar against a chilling east wind. As he walked there was no motion of the body above the waist. The arms hung immobile, with the torso as inflexible as the effigy of a lay figure.

In his enigmatic character he has been compared to the Sphinx. From the enigma standpoint the comparison is inexact; but like the Sphinx, he seemed to look out with unseeing eyes upon a world which held no glow, no surprises. Desert sand blown by the winds, dust—endless, tantalizing dust.

The photographers do him a disservice in softening the lines of his face. The lines are the most characteristic thing about his physiognomy. The tight-lipped mouth was more than a thin line or gash across the face. It dipped in sharp furrows at the corners. One finds the same dip in the jaws of a bulldog or a snapping turtle; creatures that, having taken hold, continue to hold. There are lines of concentration, too, puckering up between the sandy eyebrows, crow's-feet radiating from the corners of the eyes, lines which were born of amusement with the world rather than with the pain of it.

He seldom laughed out loud, but a thousand times I have seen him laugh with his eyes. The wrinkles came when he was amused. As to clothes, he was always well dressed; but he was not what you might call a natty dresser; he was neat; he was inconspicuous. The dean of his wardrobe was a severe, high-crowned derby hat, set on an even keel and never by any chance adjusted to a rakish angle; a serviceable hat withal, doing duty at the golf links as well as on Main Street.

As far as I know, there was no particular call to dress up for any great occasion. He was rarely seen in any Northampton drawing-rooms. He simply hadn't the time for it. As mayor, he had the privilege of a free box in the Academy of Music, one of the few municipally run theaters in the world; but he seldom appeared in person as a patron of dramatic art. He liked the theater, but there was always something else that pressed for his attention.

Whether or not it is this droop at the corners of

the mouth, there is something in his physiognomy that proclaimed the fighting man.

As a balm to baffled hopes, the boys had me sent out to St. Louis as a delegate to the national convention which nominated Alton B. Parker and Henry Gassaway Davis. A delegation from a southern state had seats immediately behind us. One of the members, a perfect child of Nature, with a fund of homely wisdom, kept nudging me and asking what it was all about. When Judge Parker was nominated a great banner was run up displaying the engaging lineaments of our stand-ard bearer. My friend's reaction was most surprising.

"We've nominated the wrong man!" he lamented.

"What's the matter? Is he too conservative for you?"

"No, it ain't that. The folks down our way are conservative. We all believe in hell, calomel and the Democratic Party. I jest don't like the man's looks."

"What's wrong with his looks? He's handsome enough."

"Yes, but he can't win. He's got a face like a sheep. There ain't no bite in his face."

Calvin Coolidge has bite in his face; a fighting,

stoic, enduring quality, the set jaw of the man who sees it through.

Young Coolidge always appeared to me to have a mighty poor time in life. Never learned to dance or play cards; music had little appeal for him. He evinced about as much interest in the pretty rosy-cheeked college girls as modern youth would display in a sprinkling of cheap automobiles on the public highway. This was not because he disliked women, but because he was shy. He held women in reverential awe as mysterious superior beings. He was the devotee who worshiped from afar.

Neither in college nor in Northampton did Coolidge ever learn to play. For one thing, he did not have the time, nor, I think, did he have the disposition. We got him to join the Warner Meadow Golf Club and he struggled to display a little spontaneous interest in the game. I remember so well the observation of a lusty young player who sat weary and dejected on the club veranda.

He remarked wearily, "I have just played a round with Cal Coolidge and feel as tired as if I had come in from a twenty-mile hike. He keeps his eye on the ball all the time and tries so hard. It is not that he plays such a rotten game of golf, but that he does not know what play is. He makes work out of it."

Later on, in the White House, Mr. Coolidge learned to enjoy music a little and was willing to concede that beauty enriches life and furnishes an escape from the pressure and tedium of business affairs. He has learned to play, though he still makes a laborious exercise of play. One finds him in the Black Hills togged out in woolly chaps, a flaming shirt and the high-heeled boots of a cowboy, or tricked out in eagle feathers and the skins of wild animals as leading Eagle of the Sioux Tribe. In the steady drizzle of the rainy season in northern Wisconsin he braved the elements and the gadflies to taste the pleasures of outdoor life. In his five-gallon hat he roamed the Virginia hills to kill quail which skilfully avoided being killed. Yes, he manfully learned to play, though he takes his play a little sadly. As Walter Bagehot observes about the Londoner, "His idea of a holiday is a fatiguing journey into the country and back."

The love of play was not bred in the Coolidge blood, and he could no more affect to be frolicsome than he could affect to be anything else he was not. Life, I fancy, was pretty sterile of amusements in the Vermont hills fifty years ago. I imagine that small-town life at Plymouth was not so very different from our old-time life on a southern plantation. There were no public games such as football or baseball; community consciousness on the social side was still in its swaddling clothes. Group social affairs always had an ecclesiastical setting, Children's Day, Sunday-school picnics, church suppers. Our delights on the plantation grew along with the close of the year. Hog-killing time, the squeals of the victims heard in the chilly dawn, the pallid bodies gammoned and hanging on their rude gibbets till nightfall. Christmas drawing on with holly, mistletoe and the ecstatic bursting of dried hog bladders to the accompaniment of firecrackers in the early morning.

Occasionally outside talent lured us to an evening entertainment in the village some six or seven miles away, the elocutionist who repeated with detestable sweetness James Whitcomb Riley's *Old Sweetheart of Mine*. An occasional musical treat featured the Swiss Bell Ringers. Simple, unaffected joys, but how tepid as compared with the thrilling amusements of the present day! We have never been able to catch up.

We medievalists don't understand the thrill of the baseball fan. Chinless and craven in the daily task as he draws forth a salted fish from the mackerel barrel at the behest of a customer in the corner grocery store; but on the ball field, transformed into the dominating male, cynical, majestical, assessing the merits and demerits of the contending players. His passion stirs him to lyric outburst. Passion-fed illusion it may be, but the passion of those who learned to play in their youth.

To many a man life would seem poor, indeed, if uncrowned by the glory of beauty—music, poetry, art, the changing colors on land and sea. Was young Coolidge really blind to beauty, dead to the enchantment of women? Or did he really see life in better perspective than the most of us? Had he something more important to think about? Was he like Saint Bernard, who fared along the shores of lovely Lake Leman with his eyes bent upon the neck of his mule lest his thoughts be diverted from the contemplation of sin, death and judgment to come by the exquisite beauty of the landscape about him?

One June evening we went trolley riding. There were no automobiles in those days. It was the day after college commencement. One feels let down after such occasions. We scrambled into a front seat and it was nice and cool bowling along in the open car across green meadows, by the shining river, and then up, up the heights to Mountain Park on the crest of the hills. Within the band played, peanut roasters hissed, humanity giggled and screamed on flying horses and roller coasters.

The carnival spirit reigned. No word had been spoken by either of us since we left Northampton. My companion at last broke into speech—"I guess we have had about enough excitement without taking in any shows." So we climbed aboard a returning car.

Speeding homeward, we halted on a turnout to let a south-bound car go by. The five-minute pause in the soft, quiet June night. The dim outlines of the river, the green hills, the grassy meadows bathed in moonlight, the scent of wild grape, the flit of little winged things in the air, faint pipings in the grass, life palpitating about us, a world of beauty—aching beauty. To my stricken fancy, the beauty of the entire universe was symbolized in a slender, *printanière* creature who had appeared the day before in the college graduating class, ethereal, clothed in filmy white raiment with roses in her hands. The very thought of her insulated me entirely from the tediums of a commonplace world. It was my firm intention to seek her out some day, to impress her; yes, I would captivate her by the allure of some fine achievement, by my brilliant talk. A querulously discordant note from my companion jarred me out of the splendid reverie.

"I have been kind of counting up the amount of

labor and material such as cross-ties, rails, poles, copper wire, to say nothing of rolling equipment, that have gone into this line. Some of our folks think we ought to strike for a nickel fare to Mountain Park. It's good politics to agree with 'em but I can hardly see it that way," he rasped disconsolately. "Just as a matter of fairness, looks like the road is entitled to a chance to make a living just the same as you and I."

Ye gods, what a man! Brooding over cross-ties and trolley equipment in moments that should have been dedicated to beauty, mystery, romance.

But the lady of my dreams passed me by in life as Beatrice once passed Dante without speaking. The memory of her faded with the years. Long afterward I met her by chance. Plumpness had descended upon her as lava overwhelms a doomed city upon a fair mountain slope. The springlike quality had entirely evaporated. She of the deliciously baffling reticences had become vocally incessant with the years. My brilliant talk was limited to tepid interjections, "Yes, indeed!" "Oh, really!" Any cretin could have made as good a showing.

Not so long after the Mountain Park excursion the unromantic Coolidge married the most charming girl in town. I remember Grace Goodhue vividly, hardly out of her teens when she came to

Calvin Coolidge as the author first knew
him some thirty-two years ago

Grace Goodhue as the author knew her
before her marriage to Mr. Coolidge

Northampton to teach in the Clarke School. A creature of spirit, fire and dew, given to blithe spontaneous laughter, with eager birdlike movements, as natural and unaffected as sunlight or the sea, a soul that renders the common air sweet.

What did she see in him?—everybody asked. Certainly no Prince Charming or knight in shining armor. She saw, let us believe, as by swift divination that unseen thing which we call, for want of a better name, character. As by revelation, she apprehended what had to be beaten into the heads of the rest of us. This much I am now willing to concede—that straight thinking about the real problems of life, even though it be in terms of railroad cross-ties and overhead charges, has its place as well as romantic mooning over unrealities on a silvery night in June.

Of the many Coolidge myths, none has had more persistent vitality than the legend of his invincibility in politics. Never beaten in a political fight, so the saying goes. In his early fights he was beaten repeatedly, whether fighting for himself or his friends. He was beaten by a young Irishman named Kennedy, in a three-cornered contest for a place on the school board. Later Connor defeated him in a fight for city solicitor. It was said later that he had wanted Kennedy to win.

After nearly ten years of battling he won his fight for mayor in a city which was nominally Republican, after a bruising contest, by only one hundred sixty-five votes. He had a great deal to contend with from the very outset. He came to Northampton a stranger, with neither money, prestige nor influential friends—naturally we underrated him. He had in opposition a gifted young man of Irish extraction, Bert Connor, just out of Yale, a magnetic personality with a genius for making friends, a gift for organization and a most persuasive tongue.

Up to the time that Coolidge was elected to the city council in 1899, no one in the Democratic camp thought it worth while to pay any attention to him; but when in the following year he was elected city solicitor it looked as if we would have to beat him to keep him in his proper place. Not being prepared to give up our political liberties and live thenceforth under an autocratic form of government, we accordingly made a great fight on him in 1901. There were whisperings, confabulations, dark conspiracies aplenty, and withal a plenty of scientific, intelligent strategy. We had a card index of four thousand electors—a Who's Who cataloguing each voter according to friends, enemies, sympathies, antipathies, accessibility.

The Coolidge chief lieutenant was Ernest Hardy, a lawyer by profession. Hardy possessed many engaging qualities which Coolidge lacked. No man was more perfectly designed by Nature for chieftainship of the Amalgamated Organization of Boosters throughout this broad land of ours. As a mixer, booster extraordinary and militant go-getter, Hardy was exemplar and prototype of our modern red-blooded, two-fisted, forward-looking, one hundred per cent. he-man. His world was the man's world of a Pullman car smoking compartment. In 1902 the Coolidge-Hardy offensive was thrown for a loss when Bert Connor was elected city solicitor.

The year before, for some mysterious reason, probably as serio-comic relief from the tediousness of being a pedagogue, I had set my heart on being elected an alderman in the city government. My opponent was Rob Weir, Coolidge's fellow lodger on Round Hill. Now politics is an uncertain game, but Connor and I had politics worked out to an exact science—an exact science enables one to predict exactly what is coming to pass. Weir apparently was attending strictly to the business of providing food for the Clarke School and we were filling the world with our fury at nocturnal gatherings in which the principles of true democracy were expounded. We went about the thing in the spirit of crusaders and our meetings betook almost the character of evangelism. It seemed almost unfair to press our manifest advantage. It was pleasant to have some obscure truck driver whisper words of praise and encouragement:

"Perfesser, you sure got them going. After you get tired being alderman, we'll make you mayor. We may get you in Congress some day."

But no meat is too strong to feed a political delusion of grandeur, and when the count actually disclosed that Weir had beaten us we could not understand it at all. Evidently there was some trick about it, just as when one is beaten at a game of checkers by moves that are not allowed by the rules. I thought at first we had been beaten by Harry Field having taken a hand. Field was formidable enough—good-looking, highly intelligent, resourceful. Coolidge had studied law in Field's office. We found, however, that Field hadn't bothered himself about the matter—that the trick had been turned by Coolidge. Later I came to receive a very adequate explanation of the mystery. Coolidge had been working behind the scenes while we were holding the spotlight in the center of the stage.

Long afterward I learned the Coolidge method. Our Democratic stronghold was Ward 1, full of fighting men of Irish stock who were born to be Democrats, but who acquired the habit of casting their votes for Coolidge. The thing was worth looking into. We went to Phil Gleason, a herculean blacksmith and a power in ward politics.

"Phil, they tell us you voted for Coolidge. Thought you were an old-line Democrat."

"So I am and always will be, but I just figured how Coolidge was about the best Democrat we had in the city. He calls himself a Republican, but I vote for him because to me he's a Democrat."

Johnny Prokup, who ran a lunch wagon, dropped away from us; John Dewey, the tavern keeper; Ed Lynch, the brick-mason; Jim Lucey, the shoemaker; all Democrats, true and tried. We went to Jim Maloney, the baker.

"Jim, is it true you have gone over to Coolidge?"

"Well, it is this way; I'm a Democrat, true and tried; but my old aunt took sick one night and was about to make a die of it. She wanted her will wrote and I was hurrying up-town about eleven o'clock to wake up Bert Connor when I met Cal Coolidge on the street. Being in a big hurry, I asked him to come over to the house and draw up the will. He got the blanks out of his office and come trottin' along. He wrote the will, got it signed and witnessed. The old lady, who was always a little close about money affairs, asked him how much he was charging. He thought a while and said, 'Well, I guess five dollars will about cover it.' She thought it would be twelve or fifteen dollars and died happy over the saving she had made. The boys got to talking about it at the wake and we decided the next time we got a chance we would give Coolidge a little lift."

We asked Cliff Lyman, from Bridgeman's bookshop, why he was against us.

"Well," he said, "I'm for Coolidge for personal reasons. I have been wrapping up books for twenty-two years, and he dropped in one day and sort of took an interest in the way I wrapped up books. He showed me how to do up a book in a neat package so there would be no bulge in the wrapping paper and make it easy to write the address on the outside. I thought that was mighty kind of him to take an interest in what I was doing and I felt like helping him."

These, in brief, are the methods by which Coolidge won through in city politics. The little way in which the modest city saw his deeds was small as compared to the ampler world of state politics to which he was translated, but I can not help but feel that his methods remained the same. Sparing of promises and money, but winning his way to the confidence and respect of his fellow mortals. We could never discover that he ever promised anybody anything or that he ever exacted a promise of political support in return for a personal favor. He fought fair, but fought with amazing resourcefulness and energy.

It seems that I must have been a glutton for punishment. Two or three months after Coolidge blasted our aldermanic ambitions, some of the boys suggested that matters might be evened up by laying him out in public debate. The proposition seemed reasonable. I had been interclass debater in my sophomore year at Princeton and again in the big senior contest. Calvin Coolidge, sparing in words, was sized up as a third-rater in public speaking.

The affair was pulled off by a semi-sporting organization known as the Rod and Gun Club. The hall was packed. We each had an opening round, with Coolidge clearly at a disadvantage. My closing argument had been spoken. I felt there was not much left to be said. My opponent, sitting in inscrutable solemnity, rose and in his most funereal manner practically laughed me out of court. Even those of us who knew he possessed a fund of dry humor did not suspect that he could ever use it to such crushing advantage.

He mournfully referred to my eminent qualifications for running the politics of a Republican city in a New England state. Nature had perfected me for the task. I was from the South; I was a Democrat; my profession was teaching girls about Attila the Hun and Theodoric the Ostrogoth.

"To establish his fraternal relationship with the Rod and Gun Club he cites his exploits in deep-sea fishing on southern coasts. Proficiency in fishing increases with the square of the distance. Has he ever so much as landed a yellow-bellied punkinseed minnow in Massachusetts waters? I doubt if our friend would be here at all," he whimsically proclaimed, "if our Massachusetts law against short lobsters was strictly enforced."

Twenty years ago the term "lobster" possessed about the same meaning in marine metaphor that "poor fish" connotes to-day. The crowd guffawed. So the sport went on. I don't remember all the dry jests, but I do remember the uproarious laughter and the sickening conviction of defeat.

There are many ways of disposing of an antagonist, such as cleaving his skull with a meat ax, running him through with a stiletto or following the methods of Joab, captain of the host, who, having conducted Abner, son of Ner, out by the gate "to speak with him quietly" smote him under the fifth rib. The Coolidge method in this particular trial of strength savored neither of brutality nor treachery, but of the curious indirect method of extermination by ridicule. At the close of the debate friends sought to administer balm to the wound. "You had him, Perfesser, till he got dry on you"—dryness in the New England dialect of the day denoting facetiousness. Yes, dry, desiccatingly dry; as dry as the devastating sirocco sweeping north from the Sahara Desert and blasting tender vegetation to its roots. People ask if Calvin Coolidge possesses a sense of humor. I reply that he does. "He jests at scars that never felt a wound." I can remember how he used to chuckle over things in our small circle at Rahar's Inn.

One night after we had finished supper the professor of logic at the college submitted a problem for our elucidation. He was an Englishman by nativity, with a broad accent and a luxuriant black beard; a dear lovable man who was always wrestling with some profound problem in metaphysics, as simple and naïve as a child about the commonplace affairs of a workaday world. He drew a line on the table-cloth with the tine of his fork.

"Let us grawnt," he posed, "that the initial point

on this line represents Rahar's Inn; the final point my lodging, which I shall soon seek by the shortest route. You will grawnt also that a straight line represents the shortest distance between two points."

"Oh, yes, yes! All that is granted. Spring it, spring it!"

"You will grawnt that a line is made up of an infinite number of points," he continued inexorably. "Further, you will have to admit that each one of these points represents a position. It must be conceded that it is impossible to occupy two positions in space at a given time. That being true, how can I occupy an infinite number of positions in a finite time? In other words, how shall I ever be able to traverse the distance from Rahar's Inn to my lodging?"

Somebody remarked jocosely, "Oh, well, I guess you will make it unless you get drunk. In that case we will send you home in a hack."

The professor withdrew in a huff. Four drovers attending the Hampden County Cattle Fair sat at the next table. They had been intrigued by the demonstration of what logic could do.

One of them broke out, "If that fellow with the bunch of black spinach on his face has got good sense, then I am crazy."

The next day we repeated this criticism to our professor of logic as we again sat at meat together. He pondered it deeply and finally proclaimed:

"Yes, I can quite well understand how the un-instructed mind would find itself wholly unable to grasp the points in my argument, but for the life of me I cawn't understand his allusion to the spinach."

Whereupon the corners of Coolidge's mouth drew down in convulsive twitchings. Twenty-three years later, when I met him at the White House, there was precisely the same downward twitching when we reviewed the effects of the logical demonstration upon an honest Hampden County cattle-breeder.

It is said of Von Moltke that he could be silent in seven languages. Calvin Coolidge, as I knew him, could be silent in at least one. Fundamentally, his quality of silence was only another phase of his instinct for frugality. The logic is clear enough; a man who is naturally frugal in expenditure, whether for dress, food or amusement, will be frugal in the expenditure of speech.

Mr. Coolidge has always been bashful. This, too, helps to explain his reticences. Though silence may sometimes be an evidence of mental vacuity, there simply being no ideas to express, in the case of Mr. Coolidge silence reflects the habit of concentration. He was always reflecting on something, turning over something in his mind. Considering the awful brevity of human life and the magnitude of the tasks to be accomplished, silence may be employed as a weapon for the conquest of time. It is a short-cut to an objective, saving detours. Certainly not a winning, electioneering quality in a back-slapping, declamatory, atta-boy age. For a great executive, however, silence may serve better than a fatal gift of fluency.

Mr. Hoover is a silent man, with a gift for concentrated reflection. He can take the abounding raw material of a particular problem and extract from it all that is valuable, as an ounce of gold may be milled from a ton of ore, and hand it to you in a minimum number of words. I have never known Mr. Hoover to ask a general question. He asks questions to which direct and specific answers may be given, provided you are clever enough to know the correct answers.

It is somewhat the same with Mr. Coolidge. Returning from Europe after five or six years of economic investigation, friends ask, "Well, how is the situation in Europe?" The question is so general as to make any reply absolutely worthless, inasmuch as Europe is made up of divers peoples and nationalities and governments. In some the governments are bankrupt and the people prosperous. Some countries are sound and not prosperous; some are prosperous and not sound, and so on. Fruitless, endless discussion about the general situation. Waste of time, talk, talk, talk, nothing settled, no valid conclusions. I noted on meeting Mr. Coolidge after nearly a score of years that he made no general inquiries such as, "How did you like it over there?" or, "Do you think Europe is recovering?" or, "What's the prospect for another warlike outbreak?" But he did ask me a great many specific questions—"How is it that the Danes can turn out bacon which sells for five or six cents a pound more than ours in the London market?" "What kind of flour do the British bakers prefer?" "Will Russia be a factor this year in the international grain trade?"

The Coolidge quality of silence unless he had something specific to say had rather a charm for me. It made him easy and comfortable to get along with. You could sit with him on a three-hour train ride from Northampton to Boston and really enjoy his companionship although he never said anything. With almost any other man you would have had the fidgets, the quietness would have become tense. But with him quietness was never assumed; it was as natural as breathing. And the queer part of it is that he was always seeking out companionship even though he did not want to talk. He always seemed to be a lonely man. If there were ten vacant seats in a railroad car, he would walk disconsolately down the aisle, seeking an acquaintance, sidle into the seat with him and relapse into solemn silence.

There are those in the world who talk and those who get things done. Connor as city solicitor reviewed the year's record of eleven cases in four printed pages of the annual report. This was considered the irreducible minimum of brevity. Coolidge reviewed his year as city solictor in two pages covering fifteen cases. A man craving the stark truth of things can't be fed with rhetoric and metaphors. He was frugal with adjectives as a miser with money. Such words as "frightfully," "awfully," "splendid," "fascinating," had no more standing with him than if they were alien terms brought over from the Coptic. His speech was about the run of mill, but shorn of all extravagances and objurgations. Powerful cuss words invoked by politicians as an intellectual means of meeting great crises had no place in the Coolidge vocabulary. He even eschewed the feebler New England diaconal oaths such as "by heck" and "by cracky." He swore not at all. I never heard him tell a vulgar story. He possessed what Jeremy Taylor calls "the prudent endearment of moderate speech."

In speech, as in aught else, there is a strength in moderation. A quiet man with quiet clothes so like the protective coloring of an animal that they merged perfectly with his environment and made no impression upon you whatever. If he took a vacation it was always a quiet vacation. His marriage was described in the local paper as a quiet wedding with no attendants. In the old days all was quiet along the Connecticut just as all came to be quiet along the Potomac. Quietude in a clamant world; imperturbability in the turmoil of our great human ant hill.

The art of politics is the art of carrying elections, which in turn is the art of so commending oneself to the public that the voter will eagerly enter a booth and firmly inscribe a perfect cross mark in a little box on the ballot opposite one's name. In these latter days Mr. Coolidge is given various ratings for political proficiency. Some folks hold to it that he is a mighty smart politician. Others will tell you that his talent for making political blunders is nothing less than a crime.

To play any game one must go according to the

political advantage, history contains no record of it. There was something about him, however, even in his younger days, that inspired confidence and respect.

Dr. Clark Seelye, whose judgment and character are built into Smith College, the largest woman's college in the world, said of Coolidge, "I never knew a man to make sounder decisions. In politics he is guided instinctively by what he believes to be right rather than by any political advantage that he may hope to obtain."

I once heard a lowly ox driver cracking his whip over the back of his beasts shout to a passing automobile driver:

"I ain't much on flashiality, but I'm great on durability."

Durability as opposed to flashiality. Lowfalutin as opposed to highfalutin notions. This is a big country with all kinds of people in it. Flashiality has its attractions, but the men whom we turn to in positions of trust, whether public officials, bank presidents, engine drivers or deacons, are men of durability rather than flashiality.

Coolidge luck! I never observed that he had any particular luck in the seven years I was thrown with him. He worked hard for what he got, and I could not then or since see any broad foundation of his success except the public confidence in him. Now a streak of luck may excite the admiration or even the envy of the public, but not its confidence. The little way in the modest city that saw his success was small. The broad way of his later life that saw his success was great, but the elements which contributed to his success were the same, I think, in all stages of his career. A baseball nine may win a particular contest by breaks in the game, but no team keeps on winning through an entire season and rises to first place in a league merely through luck.

Luck, whether in love, horse-racing, stock jobbing or poker-playing, does not favor any person consistently when spread over a period of twenty-five years. The law of averages works out whether computed by an insurance actuary or appraised in Emerson's *Essay on Compensation*. Nobody but a savage believes that the destiny of either an individual or a tribe is determined by blind luck.

So it was that I said good-by to Calvin Coolidge one day in front of Kingsley's Northampton drug store. There was almost a trace of warmth in his handshake and nasal benediction, "Luck to you!" That was twenty-five years ago. I next saw him in the White House, at the head of his own table, in splendid contrast to the modest little room in

Rahar's Inn where we formerly sat at meat together.
He had moved far and I had remained stationary all
these years but his attitude toward me had not
changed a particle as a result of the estranging influences of time, place and station. I naturally expected to find Mr. Coolidge much changed. After
attaining his exalted station he should, in theory,
have been distant, pontifical, Olympian. Not a bit
of it! He wanted to talk about old friends, such as
the Dragon brothers, who had conducted a barber
shop adjoining the Hampshire House in Northampton. His old attitude toward me remained the
same—in other words he had remained himself.
In Washington one gets a close-up on the egotisms
and self-appreciation of men in power. Oblivion
quickly enshrouds the names of the proud and
powerful, who, like the Ephemeridæ, have disported
themselves in their little brilliant hour, rejoicing
mightily in their fruitless lives. Where are the
snows of yesterday? The transience of human
glory! The certainty of quick oblivion! The fact
that no man is indispensable! These are considerations which too seldom enter into the question of
one's personal perspective on life. I would not say
that Mr. Coolidge "walks humbly with God," but
I do feel that few mortals in his position have ever
succeeded in retaining a better perspective on life.

It is said of Alexander the Great that at his feasts in celebration of victory, he would cause a poor sad slave to stand at his elbow and whisper: "Thou too art mortal. Thou too must die."

These years of power and place apparently had left no mark upon his manner. Renewing our conversation after the lapse of so many years Mr. Coolidge made no reference whatever to anything that had intervened since we last met. He was eager to talk; wanted to tell me all about the changes in Northampton:

"You know Warren died and his livery stable has been moved away from the lot next to the Catholic church. Professor Emerick's dead too. Lived across Massasoit Street from me. He left his family better off than we thought. Two of the four Dragon brothers who kept the barber shop are dead, Louie and Ed, but George and Duffy are still active. I had Phil Gleason, the blacksmith, come and stay with me at the White House. He has always been a good friend of mine. I have a great big history here in two volumes written by Charlie Hazen. He's made quite a name for himself writing history. Harry Field, you know, never married. Tried to tell me the last time I saw him how lonely he was, but didn't get a bit of sympathy. Could have married a dozen times if he had wanted to. Seemed as if he was always overcautious. Our big man, President Seelye, is still with us. Northampton would not be the same place without him. Bert Connor has put up a three-story building right across from the Draper Hotel. Got his own office in it on the third floor. Dick Rahar has quit serving meals in the inn since prohibition. I always thought a lot of Dick."

And so he went on, conjuring up old jokes, recalling people that I remembered only vaguely through the mists of years. He made only one reference to his change of state and that an indirect one:

"I'd like to have your two little boys come to the White House and see the animals. We've got a bunch of young rabbits that might interest them. Kind people send us puppies, kittens, queer animals sometimes—wombats and such."

I carried away an impression of boyishness and light-heartedness which I had not associated with Mr. Coolidge in his more youthful days. The years had dealt kindly with him, his face was fuller. His personality had taken on a glow, a touch of eagerness. He had mellowed with the years.

Again I saw him ten days after a tragic domestic misfortune—mortality's conquest of bright confident youth; the unlooked-for stroke; the event itself ironically illogical. We talked about the prosaic matter of Canadian wheat as used by our millers for blending with native wheat for the export flour trade. I rose to go. At the door he called me back.

"How are your two boys?" he asked. "One of my boys has gone," he remarked evenly, as if he were proclaiming a piece of news that I could not possibly have been aware of. "Yes, he put iodine on the injured place after his tennis game and none of us suspected any trouble. But there must have been something lacking in his blood. Possibly he had grown too fast. The white corpuscles lacked fighting power—could not subdue the poison. He did the best he could, but luck was against him. Even in his delirium he fancied himself leading a charge and winning his fight. He fancied this until near the end and it buoyed him up. Then came a change, a relaxation of the body and the two whispered words, 'We surrender.' He must have had some premonition, some intimation—I don't know."

He spoke as impersonally as if he were a doctor describing a clinical case before a group of young medical students. Not a word of self-pity, complaint or bid for sympathy, but to me he sat there a symbol of grief, of sorrow unassuageable, his face the bleak desolation of cold November rain beating

"Coolidge has been a stationary light for us to steer by. We are no longer children to be amused and contented by a display of pinwheels and Roman candles."

"He never rocks the boat."

"Mr. Coolidge has delivered us from the responsibility of taking care of ourselves. When it is proposed to take a billion dollars out of the Federal Treasury for Mississippi flood control nobody gets excited. This is a matter that can be safely left to the wisdom of Calvin the Good."

"To the fundamental principles in which he believes there are no exceptions."

"An essentially mediocre, small-bore man around whom a legend of greatness as a strong silent character has been built up by the newspapers."

"Coolidge possesses an instinct amounting to genius for choosing the right advisers."

Some of these estimates are negative; some of them are half-truths or glimmerings of the truth. Any one or all are inadequate as a complete explanation of the phenomenon under consideration. How can a man's upward career have been determined either by accident or by the newspapers for a period of thirty years, taking him from the dingy Solicitor's Office in the Town Hall of Northampton to the White House?

The writer's explanation of the amazing Coolidge Cult is this:

Mr. Coolidge has kept faith with the homely virtues of our ancestors. In our restless, complex, high-keyed Western civilization we can not forget the slow grim men of our early, half-starved beginnings in the wildernesses of the New World. The fundamental instinct is the instinct for self-preservation, and that instinct has made our democracy workable. That instinct tells us that we are not to be saved by pomp and show, rhetoric and luxury, but by honesty, frugality and simplicity of character. We live in an extravagant, money-spending, pampered, high-powered age. We must balance excess by moderation. Mr. Coolidge is eighteenth century—frugal, simple, honest, hard-bitten—set down in a twentieth-century age of jazz, extravagance in speech, dress, mad desire for pleasure. As a nation our craving is to be saved from ourselves. The yearning of the mass mind, whether in religion or politics, is for something to hold to—something to hold us—something to which the poor tentacles of self may cling, as we are carried along by the heedless current of the years. Not alone to the poor, the obscure, the insignificant, but to the rich and powerful comes the yearning for the shelter of a great rock in a weary land.

The proffer of the crown for another four years was put aside with the declaration: "I do not choose to run."

Was Mr. Coolidge simply following the prudential maxim of Sainte Beuve, "Always retire from affairs just a little before affairs retire from you"? But why search for some mysterious occult reason when the reason is implicit in Mr. Coolidge's character? He keeps faith with the traditions and virtues which have made us what we are, and one of these traditions, implicit in the idea of democracy itself, is the time limitation imposed on executive authority.

Appreciation of the virtues of simplicity, naturalness, frugality and honesty is not dying out in this Republic of ours. Mr. Coolidge's strength as president lay, I think, in the fact that to the great masses of the American people he is the symbol of virtues which we find easy to admire and hard to live up to. Mr. Coolidge has nothing to live up to; he is himself. Being a throw-back to the eighteenth century, he is frugal. He couldn't be anything different from his fellow mortals of the same epoch. They had to be frugal. Those sterile Vermont hills denied life to people who were not frugal.

Edmund Burke has pointed out that the strength

of an opinion may often lie in its moderation. Mr. Coolidge is sparing of adjectives. Nine-tenths of them could be deleted from our glorious English speech without limiting his vocabulary. In speech he is the conversational antithesis of the gushing débutante. He is not impatient of mediocrity. In the words of the great Apostle, he "suffers fools gladly." Mr. Coolidge has learned to live comfortably with himself. Richly supplied with inner resources he is not under necessity for groping around pathetically for a subject of conversation as does the resourceless man who must pursue a listener as a wild beast pursues its prey. Talk to Mr. Coolidge about the weather or ask him how he likes living in Washington and you will awaken only a tepid interest, but propound to him a perplexing problem of governmental administration and, to use a shopping expression, he will "wait on you instantly."

There is something pathetic about the childlike faith of the American people in their president. It is difficult for the mind to grasp an abstraction. We speak of fighting or dying for the flag. But the moment we begin to objectify our patriotism we personify it. It is easier to think in terms of personality than in terms of abstraction. Faith in government is really an expression of the universal dependence of the weak upon the strong. Sabatier, in his *History of Religion,* tells us that all religions have their origin in a feeling of dependence. Conscious of our weakness, our littleness, the awful brevity of human life, the invisible hazards which encompass our path, we supplicate whatever gods there be to protect and preserve us. This pathetic trust in government is a quality in human nature upon which politicians thrive! the idea that we may look to government to do for us what we can not do for ourselves; the childlike trust in panaceas—bread pills; the infatuation that the stream can rise higher than its source; the pitiful delusion that the inexorable outworkings of economic law can be suspended any more than the operation of the law of gravitation. Isn't this the secret of the wistful dependence at long range upon officialdom—the officialdom which the writer at short range views with disillusioned eyes? The swarm of petty bureaucrats busily important about unimportant things—officials treating serious business as trifles and making trifles their serious business. At close range one's ideals and enthusiasms break fruitlessly against the inertia, pedantry, formalism, red tape of piddling little bureaucrats with their petty jealousies, professionalisms and ponderous protected ignorance. As against this background stands out the figure of a rather color-

The house at Plymouth, Vermont, in which Calvin Coolidge was born

Rahar's Inn, Northampton, Massachusetts, where the author and Mr. Coolidge took their meals together for some four or five years

The left wing of this house on Massasoit Street, Northampton, Massachusetts, was occupied by the Coolidges after their marriage. They returned to it for a number of months after leaving the White House

less, commonplace, pinched personality, making no promises, embarking on no excursions, offering no panaceas—succeeding by virtue of every quality a popular politician should be without.

Has any man in exalted station better succeeded in preserving a correct perspective of himself in relation to the universe? No meat is too strong to feed delusions of political grandeur. As in a monarchy the Crown is the fountain of honor, so in our democracy the President is the fountain of patronage and preferment. He is surrounded by people who want something and who have a talent for telling him the story of his greatness. Eyes watch, knees bend around a throne. It is enough to change the accepted view of the earth's cosmogony by substituting self for the sun as the center of our terrestrial system. Mr. Coolidge's way as an obscure lawyer in a modest city was a narrow way as compared to the broad way of his later exalted station, but his relative position with respect to his social and political milieu remains unchanged.

The writer opposed Mr. Coolidge in one municipal election after another in Northampton, and as a member of the United States Tariff Commission has vexed him sorely. My views about the tariff are not after the similitude of Mr. Coolidge's views. But with it all I like to think that he is still my friend. Little persons who opposed and vexed President Wilson did not fare so well. Mr. Coolidge has lived up to the Kantian maxim of conduct, "Be a person and respect other people as persons."

An illustration or two of Mr. Coolidge's homely but endearing qualities may be vouchsafed.

Two or three days after the tragic death of Senator Brandegee I was dispatched by Mr. Hoover, whom I was then serving as economic assistant in the Department of Commerce, to deliver an oral message to Mr. Coolidge. Mr. Slemp, the President's secretary, made some difficulties about giving me a moment or two with the President. It was about eleven o'clock in the morning, with the antechamber of the executive office crowded with diplomats, members of Congress, and others with long-standing appointments. As an act of grace, I was slipped in to see the President, delivered the message, and backed away as far as the door, when Mr. Coolidge called me back and asked if I had seen about the death of Senator Brandegee. He then fell to discussing the obsession of the Connecticut Senator that he was headed for financial ruin.

"I had him come over a few days ago," he mused, "and tried to convince him that his friends would stand by him and that things would work out all right, but it was like arguing against a fixed idea."

Meanwhile the door to Mr. Slemp's office, which was not visible to the President's eye, was cautiously opened and I could perceive that the agonized secretary was beckoning me to withdraw. I rose for the second time and was well toward the door when, with a touch of asperity, Mr. Coolidge called:

"Why don't you sit down? I hadn't finished."

Whereupon he fell to commenting upon the eccentricities of his Aunt Sarah Pollard.

"She had the same obsession as Senator Brandegee. We would argue with her when she dropped in to see us in my father's home, but she had a fixed idea that she would die poor. Some nights when we had fried ham for supper she would slip a slice of hot fried ham off the table when she thought nobody was looking and wrap it up in a piece of paper and take it home. She really thought she was going to be in need, but it was only a notion, because as a matter of fact Aunt Sarah was very comfortably provided for. She had an income of three hundred and fifty or four hundred dollars a year."

During this recital the door would open every few seconds, disclosing the recessional gestures of the frantic Slemp.

Returning from an excursion down Chesapeake Bay on the *Mayflower*, the writer settled himself comfortably on a settee on the afterpart of the ship to enjoy without intrusion the beauty of the soft May afternoon as the stately vessel slowly steamed up the Potomac River. Here, with the shimmering river, the meadows, the near-by hills decked out in their delicate shades of green, one could find refuge from the hard practicalities of life under the dominating spell of beauty, luxury and the narcotic illusion of self-importance. "God's in His Heaven, all's right with the world," I could agree, feeling prouder and more important than the King of Siam. Mr. Coolidge, Commander-in-Chief of the Army and Navy of the United States, approached quietly (he does everything quietly) and seated himself silently by my side. He had something on his mind—not the stately yacht, eloquent of his great station, nor the shad fishers putting out their nets on the smiling river. Perhaps he was sighing for Lebanon. His thoughts were of the Vermont hills.

"These hills remind me somewhat of our country down East. But I don't see any sheep over on these hills," he rasped, with an injured droop to the corners of his mouth.

"Well, you wouldn't, because these farmers over in St. Mary's County, Maryland, have never gone in for much except corn and tobacco since Colonial times."

"But why don't they have more enterprise," he queried, "and go in for sheep-raising?"

"It's a question of inertia and the presence of countless dogs. At least half the population are negroes. They find some compensation for the lack of liquid capital in the possession of numerous dogs. Dogs and sheep don't go together."

"Somebody ought to get them either to kill the worthless curs or run dog-proof fences around their pasture lands. Now my father kept a bunch of sheep on the farm and taking it year in and year out made a good thing of sheep-raising. There was hardly a year he didn't realize anywhere from fifty dollars to seventy-five dollars clear profit on his sheep."

A good thing out of sheep-raising! Let it be observed that our sheepmen were then entering upon the seventh consecutive year of prosperity. It undoubtedly would be highly profitable for many small farmers to maintain small flocks of sheep on their farms. In the journey up the Potomac he had been thinking in terms of sheep while I had been thinking in terms of self. "How much is a man better than a sheep?" The question is rhetorical. But this much may be said, the sheep may produce its own woolen clothing without paying thirty-four cents per pound tariff tax.

[ 163 ]

I once asked Mr. Coolidge whether he was sensitive about newspaper criticism, mentioning a savage attack in a magazine which specialized in castigating the existing order. He could not recall the article at first, but finally made this pronouncement:

"I do remember that Slemp directed my attention to some such article and I did glance over it, but as it seemed to me a little unfair (pronounced 'unfire') I put it to one side for the waste-basket."

This attitude of judging impersonally criticism of himself is characteristic of Mr. Coolidge. The writer, at the request of a magazine editor, attempted to depict Mr. Coolidge as he appeared to his old Northampton friends. The manuscript as printed forms a portion of the present chapter. Naturally the manuscript was submitted to the President in advance of publication. He called me over to the White House and mildly remonstrated:

"It is hard for me," he complained, "to have an old friend who knows me well write me down as having an arid personality. Then," he continued, with a trace of exacerbation, "you say I don't know how to play."

"But, Mr. Coolidge, I'm not setting out to write a eulogy but to depict you as you were in the old Northampton days. Your personality could be fairly described as 'arid,' though your subsequent career suggests that a colorless personality may actually be more of a political asset than a colorful personality. As to your not knowing how to play, you never took up golf, skating, hunting, horseback riding, dancing or any other sport. As Mayor of Northampton you had a box in the municipal theater, but no one ever saw you there as a patron of music or the drama. If you want me to eulogize you, the thing can be done by suppressing anything that is disagreeable and emphasizing everything that may be flattering."

"Let it stand as it is," he crisply directed.

Not a word was changed in the manuscript as written except the substitution of "head" for "foot" in a line which contrasted his position at the White House dinner table with the humble board at which we sat at Rahar's Inn.

"I don't sit at the foot of my table," he pointed out, "I sit at the head of my table."

Certain qualities which would be regarded as temperamental weaknesses in any other president proved political assets in the case of Mr. Coolidge. Some unfortunates suffer from the defects of their good qualities. Mr. Coolidge profits from the good qualities of his defects. The former legend of his taciturnity and coldness has continually contributed to his popularity. The visitor ushered into his presence and hoping at best for a tepid, if not a frigid, greeting is perfectly delighted to be asked:

"When did you get to 'taown'?"

The wry smile that illuminates his face like a fitful gleam of sunshine on an Arctic landscape was worth at least an invitation to dinner from any other President, while his pallid and attenuated friendliness passes as a mark of exquisite urbanity. Mr. Coolidge would be as much out of place whispering drawing-room insincerities, insipidities and graciocities as would the Archbishop of Canterbury shooting the chutes.

Another Coolidge weakness endears him to the multitude as a human and understandable character—his irritability and impatience over trifling matters.

Most of us are badgered by picayune and insignificant matters; most of us do lose our tempers indefensibly; most of us do fret and fuss over non-essentials. To find a man subject to the same temperamental ills which we suffer is much like finding a great man afflicted with the same obscure physical malady that besets us. A community of weakness tends to constitute a bond of sympathy and friendship. Mr. Coolidge can put an infinite amount of industry and patience into analyzing some tedious problem, such as a budget estimate; a problem which possesses about the same human interest as genealogies of the ancient Hittite Kings. He can display no more sense of the value of time than an Oriental when it suits his mood to recall the eccentricities of his Aunt Sarah Pollard. But let somebody keep him waiting a few minutes over some trivial matter! If a messenger failed to return from the Department of Justice with a routine paper within a reasonable time, he got fretted, impatient, and made it clear to all and sundry that what he wanted was not excuses but results. On a trip to Chicago to address the American Farm Bureau Federation a crisis was caused aboard the train by the temporary disappearance of his overcoat. He demanded that overcoat right away. "Ah, then and there was hurrying to and fro, and mingled sighs and words that cannot be repeated!"

One recalls Louis XIV's annihilating criticism of a Minister of State:

"On one occasion he almost made me to wait."

Whether the desired thing is an overcoat or the appointment of a friend as Attorney-General of the United States he wants the thing without delay. If thwarted he pursues his ends with invincible obstinacy.

As against this quality of pettiness one may contrast the calmness, imperturbability, patience and wisdom which he applied to the big, complicated and baffling problems that were dumped daily upon his flat-topped desk. Late in the afternoon, after a day of intense application, he could throw himself down on a sofa in the Executive Office, cover his face with the newspaper and be sound asleep in two minutes. All quiet along the Potomac.

Conceding that Mr. Coolidge is not a brilliant man, has this fact proved an element of weakness or strength in his career? Van Buren, Polk, Buchanan, Pierce were intellectual pigmies as compared with Clay, Calhoun, Webster, Blaine, but they succeeded where the more brilliant men failed. The craving of the American people is not for a brilliant man, but for a safe man in the White House.

The Teutonic peoples have made haste by moving slowly. The wild passion of the enthusiasts and the fanatics for instant action generally springs from the false notion that they are benefiting the world relieving their own feelings.

Those who seek a solution don't go back far enough. Calvin Coolidge is considered no enigma in Plymouth, Vermont. Nothing in the youthful Coolidge excites the imagination of any New

Englander born before the *Maine* was blown up in Havana harbor. In his early surroundings he was a perfect and exact type of what everybody was familiar with. No nine-day wonder or puzzle to anybody. One recalls the story of the Down East Yankee who paid good money to see *The Old Homestead* back in the days when Denman Thompson played the part of Josh Whitcomb. The patron of dramatic art felt that he had been defrauded.

"Them folks on the stage," he complained sourly, "wan't no high-class play actors. They were just like our folks to hum."

In this narrative we have gone back twenty-five years in an effort to explain Mr. Coolidge. We could profitably have gone back two hundred years. Mr. Coolidge, belonging to the eighteenth century, is found in the age of mobility—light, heat and power distributed in an instant over copper wires, intelligence flashed across continents, under oceans and through the air in the twinkling of an eye; myriads of motor-cars darting to and fro on our public highways, a world on wheels, restless, avid, resistlessly pushing and struggling onward; fortunes made or lost in a day, big fees, high stakes. The riddle, the mystery, is not in Mr. Coolidge himself, but in the sheer inability to

measure the eighteenth century in terms of twentieth-century standards.

Mr. Coolidge does not know how to play. No
more did his forebears. Life was too serious a
thing. There was no time to play. The wilderness had to be subdued. A man went to church
with a rifle tucked under one arm and the Bible
under the other. The beauty of the external world
never appealed to these men; their minds were taken
up with the beauty of holiness. To them music
and art were as sunlight to the blind. In the hard
struggle for existence their esthetic instinct had
never been developed. It takes leisure to cultivate
the muses. These men, too, were sparing in speech.
Hard-bitten of fate, their lives were a protest
against extravagance in speech, in dress, in money
expenditure. Mr. Coolidge is exactly like his forebears and doesn't try to be anything different.

Until he became President Mr. Coolidge was a
man of narrow means. Now he has saved money—
a lot of money, judged by old standards.

One visualizes the cheaply built, double frame
house on Massasoit Street in Northampton, of
which one-half was once occupied by the Coolidges.
Frugality in the Northampton days was not so
much a principle as a necessity. Of course Mr.
Coolidge lived within his means, and living within

his means meant repressions of taste and the use of such nondescript furniture as might be had without committing himself to purchases on the installment plan. Yes, he lived within his means as revealed by the diminutive "parlor" with its plush furniture; the inevitable photograph album on the center table; the elaborately dressed doll with bouffant skirts perched upon the mantlepiece and an empurpled tanned animal's hide carrying the unabashed inscription in guilt letters "Compliments of the —— Hide and Leather Company."

Colonel Coolidge, the father, fell to talking of his son.

"My boy was always shy and quietlike and never put himself forward. It riles Calvin to have people show off. He was a trusty kind of a boy. Whatever I left for him to do, I never had to ask him later if he had done it. I thought when he was a boy he had the makings of a good doctor, but he told me that he did not care for doctoring particularly; all he wanted was a good education. He always attended to whatever he had in hand and I guess he is attending right now to what he has to do.

"The other day I was looking over some old papers in the attic and found Cal's cash accounts in college. Everything balanced up—two dollars and fifty cents a week for board, so many cents for newspapers and a bag of peanuts. Every cent accounted for. He never ran over his receipts."

Now surely these qualities are not unintelligible to Americans who know anything about the history of their country. Men of the Coolidge quality are the men who in its bleak, precarious beginnings made this nation. They were the hardy souls who, whether living in Virginia or Massachusetts, streamed westward, blazing trails, subduing the forest, fighting savages, conquering the wilderness.

We live in an extravagant, pampered, high-powered age; but democracy has an instinct for self-preservation and that instinct makes democracy workable. The life of this nation is a bigger thing than a formula. Our nominating conventions, our scheme of cabinet government are quite unknown to our written Constitution. Our vigorous national life displays itself in constant adaptation to the changing conditions of an ever-changing world. In our restless, complex, high-keyed Western civilization we have not forgotten the slow grim men of our early half-starved beginnings in the wilderness of the New World.

Further, Mr. Coolidge answers to the demand for emotional relief, the necessity for emotional reversal. The revivalist and the actor understand the psychology of emotional reliefs. The revivalist keys his audience up to a high pitch of emotion, to the point where men and women begin to weep. Sensing the need for comic relief, he will tell a funny story and set every one laughing. The expert vaudeville manager sees to it that sob stuff follows on the heels of the custard-pie turn, and vice-versa.

Mr. Coolidge's strength, I think, lies in the fact that to the great mass of the American people he is intelligible rather than enigmatical. He is not below them nor yet too high above them. He is not impatient with mediocrity and is understood by mediocrity. He has risen step by step in the public service just as a lad starting as a water boy for a railroad section gang works up through the entire executive hierarchy and becomes president of the road.

There's nothing new in all this to American experience. It is nothing new for our modern men to keep faith with the homely virtues of their ancestors. The roots of our great democracy strike deep into the soil of our Western world with its abounding resources and fresh opportunities. The topmost shoots like the myriads of lesser buds are fed from the same sap. There are tens of thousands of young men in this country not different in the essentials of character from the Calvin Coolidge of the Vermont hills; young men who with no hope of great achievement are content to do humbly their duty. Some of them sleep in France and others have retired to the background, ready, however, to come forward if danger again threatens.

# CHAPTER V

## Mussolini and the New Italy

Pragmatism judges the worth of an idea by its workableness, or, in terms of the market, by its cash value. The idea of Santa Claus is false but it is good enough to be true. For young children it is true. The true is whatever proves to be good. The pragmatist looks forward rather than backward. For him this changing world is continually unfolding. Development, whether in the individual or the mass, requires ceaseless adaptation and readaptation to the changing conditions of an ever-changing world. Ancient formulas, outworn faiths must yield to the demands of a newer and better civilization.

In bethinking myself to set down impressions of Mussolini and his works I classify him as a pragmatist and divide my text, after the manner of fledgling theologians, into four heads: first, The Man; second, The Problem; third, The Method; fourth, The Results, to which possibly may be added a brief epilogue as to the cash value of Mussolini's ideas and the price the Italians must pay for the values thus bestowed.

As to the man, I have known him both high hat
and hatless; on the stage, off the stage. Like King
David of Israel, who danced before the people, he
dramatizes himself in public, enacting the rôle of
mighty Cæsar or the indomitable Napoleon. On
the stage he wears a mask, he struts, he attitu-
dinizes. One moment the cold and taciturn in-
trovert, the next the man of persuasive rhetoric, as
impassioned as Savonarola. In private he can be
as soft as velvet, ingratiating, exquisitely cour-
teous, exhaling charm as a flower exhales its perfume. One is amazed at his plain speaking, his
unaffectedness. Conversing with him in private
he seems, above all things, natural, without pose,
kindly, sincere. In public utterances a dogmatist
but in the innermost recesses of his cave, the Chigi
Palace, elastic in thought and feeling. Is this the
art that conceals art? Does he wear a mask in private as in public? Like the Apostle, is he all things
to all men? Some reckon him an opportunist, but
this disposes of his many-faceted personality too
easily.

Son of a blacksmith he is the prototype of
the many-sided Italian geniuses who surpass their
fellow creatures not in one but in many arts. Leonardo da Vinci, engineer, musician, painter. The
versatile Leon Battista Alberti, prodigious athlete,

musician, architect, physicist, writer of authoritative books on a dozen subjects. Of the same type Benvenuto Cellini, Michael Angelo.

As to Mussolini's political principles. Does he have any? He has been socialist, republican, atheist, pacifist, everything that as Dictator of Italy he is not. He's not an opportunist, he is a pragmatist. Pragmatism is not so much a body of doctrine as a method for getting things done. This many-sided intellect has worked out a novel method for getting things done. The worth of his method lies in the success of its application. Mussolini's method works. His ideas turn out to have a priceless cash value for the Italy of his day. It happened that Italy in the dark years succeeding the war produced a man who, striking out along bold and original lines, rescued the country from chaos and disintegration.

One asks why a great people wedded to principles of individualism and popular government consent to have free institutions set aside at the behest of any person or party. The answer lies here. They have chosen the lesser of two evils. We shudder at autocracy but mobocracy is worse. Some armies have been successful when led by a bad general, but no army can be successful when led by a debating society.

The writer lived in Italy through the worst years succeeding the armistice. One's general impression of the black years 1919, 1920 and 1921 were slackness—endless, tantalizing, heartbreaking slackness. Tens of thousands of soldiers still in uniform turned their hands to no useful account. Five tax-eating men were employed by the State railways to do the work of two men. The country swarmed with beggars. Chaos, disorder, poverty, discontent reigned. A tramcar comes jolting along crammed with passengers. It halts. Thirty individualists rush the car. They jam the car platforms without giving insiders the slightest chance to alight. After much delay the passengers escape through the windows. Inert policemen stand indifferently by. Who cares! The war has been won; everybody has a license to go to hell by the shortest route he may choose. Electric lights fail when one sits down to read in the evening. Electric cars stall for lack of power and one walks home. *Manca corrente* (lack of juice). Lack of juice, lack of coal, lack of bread, worst of all lack of discipline. In these years Italy could have supplied ten terrestrial globes with hurdy-gurdy players, the operation of the instrument appealing to two prevailing passions—love of music and love of leisure. If a man had accumulated enough to own a modest automobile he was like to be assaulted with sticks and stones and screams of *"pescecani"* if he drove abroad in the land. *Pescecani,* meaning dog-sharks, was the cant term of reproach liberally applied by those who had not to those who had. The treatment of automobile owners I secretly rejoiced in since these proud fellows in the exercise of human liberty opened their cut-outs and honked their horns most devilishly at any hour of the night in ascending any one of the seven hills of imperial Rome.

The sabotage of every pleasure car would have been an act of retributive justice.

And talk! No limitations except the necessity of a listener. The country was swept by an epidemic of *cacoethes loquendi, scribendi, carpendi,* that is to say, a morbid desire to harangue, to scribble, to find fault. Disturb an ant-hill and observe the agitation of its occupants. Confused, they run frantically helter-skelter, doubling back and forth, stopping an instant to touch mandibles. Italy, the great human ant-hill, had been grievously disturbed by the war. What to do! What to do! Well, every mother's son of them had ideas or germs of ideas. These ideas or near-ideas clamored for expression. The Italian is gifted above any other race in the arts of vocal expression. The country is populated with inglorious, pigmy Salvinis, Duses; millions of miniature human Vesuviuses and Etnas in vocal eruption, accompanied by shrugs, gesticulating hands—supplicatory, expository, imprecatory hands. The Chamber of Deputies in one respect was a true representative assembly. Gesticulating deputies emphasized, scolded, resented imputations, hissed, laughed to scorn in frenzied, ululating, screaming oratory until Mussolini came along and, like Cromwell ejecting the Rump Parliament, "put an end to their silly prating." Every man exercised not only the God-given liberty to talk but license to act. One strike after another disheartened and demoralized the business enterprises of the country. Industries were taken over by the workers and operated for the benefit of organized labor. It gave one a shock to observe the red flag of communism flying about great industrial establishments such as the Fiat Motor Works at Turin. Of course Italian Labor found itself incapable of presiding over Industry, and soon began to realize that it was better to be a directed workman with pay than to be an undirected boss without pay. Even the labor organizations began to split up. Individualism gone mad was reflected in the national parliament with its dozen or more mutually antagonistic factions.

Factionalism has been the historic weakness of the Italians since the downfall of the Roman Empire. Italy was split, after the fall of the Empire, into jarring, contending, rival states. Despotism was the only possible government for these jangling, contending Ishmaelitish broods. Read the record of the wars between the Pisans and Florentines and along with it the history of the factional fights among the Pisans and the Florentines. The golden periods in Italian history have been associated with splendid despotisms such as that of Lorenzo in Florence, Leo in Rome. Each state was marked by its own political genius and trade physiognomy. What peculiar conditions in the fifteenth century made the Genoese sailors, the Venetians Levant merchants, the Perugians captains of industry, and the Florentines bankers? For fifteen hundred years political unity has been the great desideratum of the Italians. Liberty having degenerated into license, the country three years after the armistice presented a striking illustration of parliamentary and electoral degeneration.

"Men," says Mussolini, "are perhaps tired of liberty. They have had enough of it. Other watchwords exercise a much greater fascination on the youth of to-day—order, hierarchy, discipline."

If it is asked why a great people consent to part with local self-government, freedom of speech and of assembly one answers that they renounce the lesser for the greater good.

"The people do not want liberty," declares Mussolini. "They want railways, bridges, drains, houses, roads, water and light."

The Italians want *things*. Forty-two million human beings are pent up within a narrow peninsula no greater in area than the state of California. Mouths to be fed—bodies to be clothed. After the sacrifices of the war their disillusioned souls longed for the good things of this life as they never longed before. Bodies can't be fed and clothed by rhetoric, formulas, abstract political theories.

The Italians are a poor folk set down in a land destitute of the prerequisites of modern industrialism. Nature has dealt in a niggard fashion with the land. There is no abundant native wealth, either on the surface of the soil or beneath it. Italy produces no raw cotton, petroleum, or copper. Her iron resources are strictly limited. Her scanty forests have been cut to pieces. The country is without navigable rivers. The adjacent seas are but meagerly stocked with fish. Not a pound of good steam coal has ever been discovered in the kingdom. Italy is the least self-contained of all the great industrial countries of the world. Successful industrialism largely depends upon the juxtaposition of iron and coal. Italy must look to foreign sources for forty per cent. of the food she eats, for fifty per cent. of the lumber and steel used in construction, and for practically all the coal, copper and raw cotton employed in her industrial life. The Italians, considering their slender resources, suffered intolerably from the war. Fully a half-million robust young men were left dead on the field of battle. The net direct war cost exceeded twelve billion dollars, or fully half the direct war expenditures of this country. Italy's total wealth at the beginning of the war, estimated at sixteen and a half billion dollars, compared with our total of two hundred twenty billion. Italy's note circulation of slightly over two and a half billion dollars at the close of the war compares with five hundred fifty-two million eight hundred sixty thousand dollars at the beginning. The cost of living represented by the figure one hundred at the beginning of the war rose to three hundred forty-eight at the end of the war. The budgetary deficit, as well as the adverse trade balance, ran into hundreds of millions of dollars. As over against these great sacrifices of blood and treasure Italy's war gains appear pitifully small. Some barren wastes in North Africa inhospitable to colonization, some strips of Austrian territory, the valley of the Adige, and the Istrian Peninsula with its port of Trieste. Even the command of the Adriatic was denied through the award of Fiume by an American President to the Jugo Slavs.

The central fact in the Italian economy is the pressure of population on the food supply. Translated into other terms Italy needs more breathing space, more elbow room, more natural resources, a coefficient of expansion that will correspond to the rising coefficient of population.

Can the basic facts of a nation's economic life be altered artificially by Government decree?

"Ah Love! Could you and I with Him conspire
To grasp this sorry Scheme of Things entire,
    Would not we shatter it to bits—and then
Remold it nearer to the Heart's Desire!"

Who at times has not longed for autocratic power—power to smash the existing order to bits and remold it nearer to the heart's desire? Wouldn't it be a great thing to make health rather than disease catching?

How remold Italy nearer to the heart's desire? It can be done, answers Mussolini, by mobilizing the country for peace just as it was mobilized for war. In a way the problems of peace are harder than the problems of war. War is directed by a common aim—business by diverse aims. War means waste—business means saving. It is easier to waste than it is to save. Mussolini has created a new type of state capable of applying to the problems of peace the efficiency methods which are applied to the problems of war. If you want to remold human societies quickly and effectively it must be done through centralized and unified command. No army can be successfully led by a debating society. Everything depends on discipline, order, hierarchy, authority—subordination to a commander-in-chief. It is something to ask of forty-two million people that they should surrender their right to talk as they please, to write as they please, to vote as they please. After the sacrifices of the war the Italians were asking for ease, quietude, soft living. It is difficult to lead men from self-indulgence to work, discipline, renunciation. But strong men make strong creeds, and strong creeds make strong men. It is well to remember that epicureanism, the Roman philosophy of soft living, gave way to stoicism, the Roman philosophy of hard living. On the ruins of democracy Mussolini has built his guild state, the like of which the world has never seen before. He finds no fault with democracy where it can be worked. It won't work in Italy, that's all. Being a pragmatist he discards it as he would a steam-engine which won't make steam, or a telephone which won't transmit sound. For a government by the people he has set up instead a Board of Directors corresponding to the general staff of an army, Mussolini being Director General of the General Staff. This Board of Directors, stating the matter crudely, represents the organized, syndical or occupational associations of the Italians. These associations are the ground sills of Mussolini's guild state. Thus labor, capital, the industries, the professions are built into the state. Popular government is dead in Italy. No man, whether college professor or ditch digger, has any choice as to how he is governed, but he may enjoy the satisfaction of knowing that his destiny as an individual is tied in with the destiny of the nation.

"If the nation," proclaims Mussolini, "is powerful, the least of her workmen can hold his head high. If the nation is impotent and disorganized, if the country is inhabited by small disorderly people, the results are felt by everybody and all have to take on a humble, resigned attitude, as was the case for twenty years and more in Italy."

The fascist doctrine denies the dogma of popular sovereignty, and in its stead proclaims the dogma of the sovereignty of the state. Thus Italy has been rescued almost overnight from the bedlam of mob government—a government which may easily become the most detestable tyranny of all. Under the new régime the Italian localities as such no longer enjoy representation in the Chamber of Deputies. The whole kingdom has been incorporated into a single national electoral constituency. Local self-government has been replaced by *podestàs* or mayors named by the Roman Dictator.

It is one thing to destroy existing institutions and quite another thing to construct something better. It is one thing to plan the work and quite another thing to work the plan. An exhibit of how the plan is worked may be conveyed as by the little pictures peeped at in a biograph.

Italy, brought to the verge of bankruptcy by the war with an annual deficit of billions of lire, is now on the credit side of the ledger with a comfortable balance of income over outgo.

The national currency which had crashed to ruinous depths has been stabilized and now constitutes the keystone of public finance.

Mussolini has called upon falling water to redress nature's parsimony in denying coal to the country. Italy's investment in hydroelectric power has risen by four hundred per cent.

[ 187 ]

Unemployment in the country has been reduced to less than one per cent. Eight years ago the country was alive with beggars and jobless men.

Strikes are now unknown in Italy; labor organizations having been built into the state strikers are promptly jailed. The labor problem in Italy no longer exists.

Hundreds of thousands of acres of swamp lands have been reclaimed. Great irrigation projects are being put through in the island of Sardinia and in southern Italy, all marking an advance toward the solution of the country's bread shortage.

The Italian Merchant Marine has been restored to more than pre-war strength.

The former Austrian port of Trieste has recovered its old time importance, while Genoa has become the first port in the Mediterranean.

Savings bank deposits have now attained a figure of eighteen dollars per capita—small in comparison with rich America but large in contrast with pre-war Italian savings.

Italy's vast strides in industrialism are rapidly transforming the country from a purely agricultural to a manufacturing state.

The swift development of the artificial silk business in Italy constitutes an epoch in modern industrial pioneering genius. While it has taken Italy a thousand years to attain a commanding place in the production of natural silk, in the space of a decade the country has surpassed all European rivals in the fabrication of artificial silk.

Two billion lire have been put into building operations to meet the chronic housing shortage.

Beggars have been put to work, flower-beds set out, schools established, highways built, workable telephone systems installed.

So much for some of the tangibles. How about the intangibles? Mussolini presses to the lips of his countrymen the intoxicating cup of glory. Mussolini himself is necessarily a supreme egotist. The egotism of the Chief is reflected downward and permeates all grades of society. He has restored the waning confidence of the Italians in themselves. Man lives not by bread alone, he lives by his dreams, his aspirations, his vanities. Take away a man's vanity and he is defeated. He is a Cornwallis at Yorktown. Many a pauper in an insane asylum is happy in his delusions of grandeur. Material delusions of grandeur find expression in ideas of bigness, power, superiority. The ultimate test of superiority is this. "Can I kill thee or canst thou kill me?" Roughly speaking, every gain in civilization finds its expression in improved arts of killing. Military success is a matter of population plus organization. The winning combination in war is numbers plus discipline and intelligent leadership. The Italian population is increasing by leaps and bounds along with the slackening outflow of emigrants.

"The time is past," remarks Mussolini, "when new countries can be allowed to build themselves up and old nations be allowed to revivify their decadent blood with the Italian vitality which is needed for domestic development."

Are the people of Italy happier under the Fascisti régime? That is a fair question, but how measure happiness? Mussolini assures us that they are. He spoke more earnestly on this point than on any other in a thirty-five minute interview accorded the writer. The sole gesture which he made during the entire conference accompanied the declaration that he had increased the happiness of his people and would continue to do so.

"After an absence of five years from Italy," he observed, "you note on returning evidences of increased happiness and well-being. Return to Italy five years from now and you will observe even greater changes on the side of human happiness. Even the expressions on the faces of our people will have changed for the better. (*Anche le faccie seranno cambiati per migliora.*)"

In making this declaration he passed his hand over his face with much the movement of a cat washing its face with a paw after swallowing the fattest mouse in the family attic.

Opinions differ as to the increase in the sum

total of human happiness in Italy, but the weight of evidence is on the side of Mussolini's contention.

Professor Mortara, the eminent economist, insists that the Italian proletariat are worse off than before the war, but how can that be, seeing that Italian workmen are more continuously employed and at a higher rate of wages than pre-war with the government alert to enforce penalities against social injustice. Hitherto defenseless, inarticulate people are protected at every turn against exploitation. Let a tenement house owner put up rents if he dare.

The Italian bourgeoisie lost two-thirds of its investments through the war, but it always was poverty-stricken.

Italy possesses a class of educated, genteel poor aspiring to wear white collars and work at desks. This class has probably benefited less from the new dispensation than any other. Jobs have diminished; applicants have increased. Before the war there were two applicants for every white-collar job. Now there are four. The shabby genteel class, consisting of clerks, bookkeepers, human cash registers and human adding machines continue to exist upon what we would consider starvation wages. Even the top men in this class, such as bank cashiers, responsible for every soldo that passes through their hands, average no better than fifty dollars a month. College graduates and professional people fare hardly better. It is rather difficult to assess the wages of the servant class in terms of cash. The Italians are intensely individualistic. Every relation in the human ant-hill is a personal relation. No job is sought in the government on one's merits, it must be obtained through soliciting the influence of some one higher up.

Try to sell an article on its merits, one winds up by haggling on a purely personal basis. "Seeing that it is you, you may have it for so and so." One can't hire a servant to do a particular job for a stipulated sum. In addition to cash he must receive a retainer. Perquisites must be added, such as the benefaction of a pair of old pantaloons for the workman, corals for his baby, candles for the wife's Saint's Day. All this, of course, harks back to the days of feudalism and the personal relationship that subsisted between the feudal lord and his retainers.

It is clear that the Italian farmers, representing nearly two-thirds of the population, are better off under the new régime. High protective duties on imported foods assure better prices for Italian crops in the home market.

Presented to the author by Mussolini at the conclusion of an interview.
The Roman V in the inscription signifies the year of his administration

The parvenu, or new-rich class, has increased both in numbers and in the amount of accumulated wealth, though there is no class in Italy to correspond to the American millionaire class. The plutocratic class can scarcely be said to exist in Italy. Italian millionaires one encounters in Roman society can be counted on the fingers of one hand. Milan society makes a little better showing. Poverty may be said to increase with the square of the distance as one journeys from north to south in Italy. There are probably more millionaires of Italian birth in New York than Italian millionaires in the entire Kingdom of Italy. The writer recently addressed the annual dinner gathering of the Italian Chamber of Commerce at the Biltmore Hotel in New York City. President Giannini, of the Chamber, whose great fortune has been made in American banking enterprises, surveying the assembled audience of six hundred fifty banqueters, remarked, "I can point out in this audience at least thirty millionaires who came over to this country in their early years as poverty-stricken immigrants. I myself came over as an immigrant with no more than a hundred dollars in liquid capital."

I believe I can name offhand, out of personal contacts, a majority of the Italian millionaires in Italy.

Pirelli,—rubber, automobile tires, transmission cables.

Gualino—moving spirit in the Snia Corporation (artificial silk).

Volpi—hydroelectric and shipping enterprises, his start having been made in the Turkish tobacco trade.

Agnelli—Fiat automobiles.

Donegani—brains of the great Montecatini enterprise (chemicals of high and low degree).

Toeplitz—Director of the Banca Commerciale Italiana, Italy's greatest bank, interlocking with a thousand and one industrial and commercial enterprises.

Rolando Ricci—lawyer of high degree. Probably the only man in Italy who has made a million dollars and more out of the practise of a learned profession.

Florio—wine vender extraordinary.

Rossi—the world's most illustrious vermuth man.

When I dwelt in Italy the Perrone brothers had come to great estate and had a finger in a multitude of industrial pies. They crashed with the failure of the great Banco di Sconto along with the affluent Pogliani, its director. Clearly the Italians have prospered more in the past eight years than in any similar period in their recorded history of more than two thousand years. More men are at work with better pay; the productive energies of the country have expanded tremendously. Italy is passing beneath our eyes from an almost purely agricultural to an industrial nation. The low standards of living in such cities as Naples, Foggia, Lecce, Catania, Brindisi would appal the average American, but one must remember that the poverty of Italy finds its complement in the frugality and industry of the people. *"L'Inglese crepa di fame dove l'Italiano fa fortuna.* (The Englishman starves to death where the Italian waxes fat.)"

As ever in the big cities the cafés are still thronged with loungers who read newspapers, write letters and contentedly sit three hours over a three-cent drink.

No attempt can be made here to set down in detail the accomplishments of the Fascisti régime. It is interesting, however, to visualize Mussolini up against two of our toughest domestic problems, namely, farm relief and liquor control. The writer has heard more words spoken on these two topics by Washington officialdom than on any other ten, including the social status of Mrs. Gann. A Niagara flood of prescriptions, programs, palliatives, bread-pills, reversals, contradictions—the endless palaver of a nation-wide debating society with nothing accepted by the extremists as final. Here's how

Mussolini tackles the problem of farm relief: He first forms his plan; next, plans the work; third, works the plan. The Italian agrarian problem may be elucidated in terms of wheat. Alimentary paste made of wheat is the pivot around which the Italian dietary problem revolves. The central fact in the economic life of the country is the pressure of population on food supply. Italians must depend on foreign sources for more than one-third of their daily bread. Botanically, the wheat plant is a grass. Surveying the robust vigorous Italians nourished on wheat one may exclaim with the Psalmist, "All flesh is grass." The value of bread exhausts itself with its consumption, while such an import as raw cotton or steel passes into constructive channels. The quantity of imported wheat amounting yearly to say one hundred fifty million dollars in value accounts for fifty per cent. of the country's commodity trade balance. One would say that the Italian agrarian problem is easy of solution. Yes it is, if the Italians are willing to pay the price. The Italian wheat problem is ours inverted or ours turned wrong side out. Roughly speaking, Italy is a country with a paucity of natural resources and an abundance of cheap labor, while ours is a country of abundant resources and dear labor. The clue to Italy's economic position is found in scarcity of resources and super-abundance of people.

On the surface Mussolini's wheat problem seems simple in comparison with ours. Raise the Italian wheat tariff by a dollar a bushel and the Italian farmer will need no further argument for growing wheat. In America it is a question of how to deal with a surplus, in Italy how to deal with a deficit. Our problem would be solved by moving farmers from the land to the city, the Italian problem by moving townsmen from the city to the farm. Our problem is how to raise the price of wheat and keep down production; the Italian how to increase production and keep down price.

Our difficulty is over-production. The penalty for over-production is lowered price. Excess production breaks the domestic market. We reclaim swamps, irrigate semi-arid lands, perfect farm machinery and thus produce more wheat. In so doing we increase the weight of surplus wheat which hangs like an incubus over the market. We thus work at cross-purposes, pursuing objectives that are contradictory, antagonistic and mutually destructive. In truth Mussolini's objectives are just as contradictory, antagonistic and mutually destructive as our own. He would at once raise the birth-rate, increase the wheat harvest, revaluate the lire, reduce the cost of living. But you can't ask for more children, more bread, dearer money and cheaper commodities all at the same time any more than you can ordain a rise in grain prices to suit every farmer, a fall in food prices to suit every householder, a rise in wages to suit every laborer, a drop in commodity values to suit every buyer. The economist knows of no magic whereby these beautiful and desirable ends are to be secured at the bidding of the government. Still the great Italian pragmatist is making fair headway increasing Italy's bread supply. His scheme works. As a result of Mussolini's "battle of the wheat" the crop out-turn has risen from one hundred seventy million bushels in 1924 to two hundred sixty million six hundred sixty-nine thousand bushels in 1929.

Mussolini's appeal for larger families has made a profound impression.

"If," he declaims, "the population decreases we can not become an Empire. We become a colony. That is why I am helping agriculture, why I favor rural communities, why I do not wish industry around Rome, why I permit in Italy healthful industries pertaining to agriculture and the sea."

Despite Mussolini's dictum the perverse birth-rate is obstinately falling instead of rising in Italy.

Plentiful food and a rise in the birth-rate go hand in hand. The great upsurge in the British population at the time of the industrial revolution coincided with the importation of cheap grain from America. You can not put an import tax of seventy-three cents a bushel on wheat, a deficiency product, without raising the price. Mussolini has had a free hand in carrying out his agrarian problem but he has had to pay and pay heavily for his achievement. He is up against fundamental economic laws which can neither be suspended nor repealed by executive fiat. Can omnipotence itself make the part greater than the whole? The laws of arithmetic and political economy are stronger than the strength of dictators.

Now as to Mussolini's program for liquor control. I confess to be fed up with prohibition discussions, nauseated once and for all with the everlasting iteration and reiteration of time-worn clichés. But Mussolini contributes novel and piquant suggestions about liquor control. The Italians, unlike the Russians and Finns, are not hard drinkers of hard liquors. Without being drunkards they are immoderate drinkers of wine. The drink problem in Italy is fundamentally an economic problem. Here is the situation: Approximately eight and a half million acres of land are cultivated to vines, or more than half of the total acreage of all Europe in vineyards. France, standing next to Italy in point of acreage, has less than half the amount of land in vines. But France, with less than half the acreage, produces more than double the amount of wine. Another point: While France exports over two hundred fifty million gallons of wine Italy on balance imports over twenty-seven million gallons. That is to say, with the enormous acreage devoted to vine culture the Italians on balance must needs import twenty-seven million gallons to supplement their wine resources.

"Do you not agree," I asked the Italian Dictator, "that the enormous acreage given over to vine culture is a serious economic drain?"

"On the drink question, are you wet or dry?" he shot back.

This was embarrassing!

"I am personally dry *(secco)*," Mussolini went on, "in a country overwhelmingly wet. Our people drink too much for their own good," he commented, quoting a string of figures as to production, consumption, imports. "Our national consumption of wine," he continued, "is approximately one hundred liters (twenty-six gallons) per capita, but as the women and children drink but little this means a per capita consumption of over two hundred liters (fifty-two gallons) for the men. The enormous acreage in vineyards brings little or no gold into the country, since the bulk of our wine, unlike that of France, is not produced for export. Italian wines are heady, running about twelve per cent. alcohol. Our people who drink in their homes or in cafés belong to the type of moderate drinkers. Heavy drinking in Italy is associated with the *osteria,* or common saloon, where no food is served with drink. Frequenters of these low saloons, such as chauffeurs, muleteers, pick and shovel men, drink to excess. I am aiming to reduce the consumption of wine by that element of the population which uses it to excess. I see no logic in penalizing other classes of our population who use wine in moderation. We are cursed in Italy by the low-class saloons and I intend to do away with them—but gradually. My agents are instructed to keep an eye on the *osterie.* When a complaint is made about a particular saloon I close it and from my edict there is no appeal. I have closed twenty-seven thousand saloons in five years; give me time and I will close them all. When I came into power there was a low saloon for every five hundred inhabitants; we now have one to every thousand of the population. I have already reduced the per capita consumption of wine from one hundred twenty-eight liters pre-war to about one hundred liters. I deal with the drink question by making haste slowly rather than by attempting to change inveterate national habits overnight. In this matter of closing saloons I am fortunately not compelled to solicit the approval of either the saloon-keeper or his clients. All that belongs to the dark ages of democracy from which we have now happily emerged."

No ifs, no buts; none of the cant and caution of true "servants of the people."

Characteristic American comment on the Fascisti régime runs about as follows:

First, "Mussolini has done a whale of a lot for Italy, but he's pulled some rough stuff which we Americans wouldn't stand for—no, not for a minute."

Second, "Mussolini has done great things, but suppose some wild-eyed fanatic puts a bullet through him—what then? Won't his régime go down like a house of cards?"

Commenting on this latter observation, Mussolini believes or affects to believe that his Fascisti State is built on permanent foundations. He tells you quietly of what he expects to accomplish in the next five or ten years, speaking with the utmost assurance. As to the suggestion that he has completed his work and is ready to retire, I may cite the exact language he used in seeking a reason for Mr. Coolidge's historic declaration that he did not choose to run.

"What does your president mean when he says he doesn't choose to run again? Is there any legal reason that would prevent him? Is he becoming unpopular?"

"Not at all," I replied. "It seems to be a matter of personal taste."

"I can't understand it," mused the Italian Dictator. "If things were going badly with your country that would be an explanation. *Perché cambiare quando tuto va bene?* (Why change when things are going well?)"

The Fascisti government, according to Mussolini, is a great machine that having been set up is now capable of being run by leaders bred to the task. The big three at the time I discussed the matter with Mussolini were Volpi, Federazoni and Turati. Intelligent Italians with whom I talked believe that Mussolini could retire without vital shock to the structure of his government or slowing down of the processes of its administration.

The American view that we would not tolerate Mussolini's strong-arm methods in this country is correct. But are we able to visualize the conditions of poverty and demoralization in this country which prevailed in Italy at the close of the war. We accept democracy as the final word in government but it is possible that our favorite notions may be wrong, our firmest beliefs unfounded. Most of us slumber on in a state of complacent satisfaction with the institutions into which we are born, whether the Baptist Church or the Republican Party. It is upsetting to our complacency to find forty-two million people rejecting political principles which are to us sacrosanct. "One of the greatest pains to human nature," comments Walter Bagehot, "is the pain of a new idea." Less than ten years ago thousands of American boys, driven as by evangelical fervor, took up arms for what seemed the holy cause of making the world safe for democracy, but the pitiful thing about it all is that democracy does not always make the world safe for the peoples who embrace its doctrines.

Two judgments may be rendered of Mussolini and his works. Machiavelli's *Prince*, written by an Italian four hundred years ago, is a critical analysis of the political disorders of Italy, with cold scientific suggestions as to how autocratic power may be set up and maintained. Hegel, in his *Philosophy of History*, records his judgment of

Machiavelli's *Prince*—a judgment which applies in great measure to Mussolini's Fascisti régime. "This book," he says, "has often been cast aside with horror as containing maxims of the most revolting tyranny. Yet it was Machiavelli's high sense of the necessity of constituting a State which caused him to lay down the principles on which alone States could be formed under the circumstances. The isolated Lords and Lordships had to be entirely suppressed, and though our ideas of freedom are incompatible with the means which he proposes— yet we must confess that the despots who had to be subdued were assailable in no other way inasmuch as indomitable lawlessness and perfect depravity were thoroughly ingrained in them."

Machiavelli, having lost favor with the Medicean prince who autocratically governed Florence, retired to his country estate to eat out his heart in bitterness and disappointment. Mussolini tells us that there is room in Italy for Fascists and non-Fascists, but no room for anti-Fascists. Thousands of Italians whose views differ from those of Mussolini are living in exile, shorn of property, position, citizenship.

Government by an all-wise and all-benevolent despot is ideally the best form of government, only be sure that your autocrat is all-wise and all-

[ 205 ]

benevolent. Mussolini is giving the Italians what
their bodies and souls yearn for. He would be a
perfect success if he were also giving them self-
government, freedom of speech, freedom of assembly, freedom of the press. All of which recalls
Sarpi's merciless epigram on Pope Leo X: "Leo
would have been a perfect Pope had he been able to
combine with his many fine qualities some interest
in the affairs of religion."

# CHAPTER VI

## SENATOR SMOOT—DILIGENT IN BUSINESS

"Must I be carried to the skies,
On flowery beds of ease,
While others fought to win the prize
And sailed through bloody seas?"

To THE above rhetorical question of the pious hymnologist, Reed Smoot, Apostle of the Church of Latter-Day Saints, twenty-seven years United States Senator from the State of Utah, returns an emphatic negative. Mr. Smoot does not ask to be carried anywhere on flowery beds of ease. He prefers to work his own passage just as his father before him worked his passage navigating a prairie schooner over mountains and deserts to the Promised Land in the Valley of the Great Salt Lake.

The senior Senator from Utah is of tough-fibered adventuring stock—men who pushed out to the far periphery of habitable Mother Earth to pursue their destinies in peace. Pioneers in the wilderness have left their stamp upon America. As pioneers our ways have been land ways while the ways of Britain have been the great waterways of the globe itself. The covered wagon is the symbol of our rise to fortune just as a floating vessel propelled by wind and steam is the symbol of Britain's rise to greatness.

One asks why the Latter-Day Saints led by Brigham Young should have chosen a site for the Temple of Zion in an unfruitful wilderness hard by the bitter waters of an inland sea. One may ask the same question about the Land of Promise to which Jehovah led His chosen people. The Jordan of romance is a sweet and pleasant stream flowing over shining strands. The Jordan of reality is a sinuous, turbid creek threading its way through desert wastes and lined on either side with stunted wormwood scrub. Jerusalem, the Holy City, is set down in a dreary sterile waste of stones and rubble. It may be possible that the Chosen of God carry their Promised Land around with them in their own hearts. Be this as it may, we know that when the animals that drew the wagons of the Latter-Day Saints to Utah fell in their tracks from starvation and exhaustion human hands tugged at the traces and brought the lumbering, creaking wagons through to safety.

These colonists take us back to the patriarchal age when society was scarcely emerging from the tribal period of human culture. Like the Hebrew patriarchs they reverenced their God, fathered great broods of children, watched their flocks by night, waged incessant wars of defense against the Indians and cattle thieves which corresponded to the Amalekites and Jebusites of the antique world. They subdued the wilderness, reclaimed arid lands, watched and prayed. To the rationalist their stern creed is a hard saying, but the supernaturalism implicit in all religions is a "hard saying" for men who will not believe unless they know. When the Founder of Christianity began to talk to His devoted little band of followers about the supernaturalism of giving them His body to eat some rejected His teaching as a "hard saying and walked no more with Him."

Now it just happens that Senator Smoot is a true son of his forebears. They were of stoic, enduring quality. They had to be frugal and industrious. The alkali desert denied life to persons who were not frugal, industrious, lion-hearted.

As man emerges from the bare struggle for existence the instinct that early comes into play is intellectual curiosity, the beginning of all knowledge. Later emerges the esthetic instinct, or the love of beauty, the beginning of all art. Senator Smoot is surpassed by no statesman of the present generation in his intellectual curiosity. Like

Browning's grammarian his passion is not so much to live as to know. But his esthetic instinct still remains undeveloped. A man engaged in digging an irrigation ditch has no time to rhapsodize over the delicate cloud tints of the setting sun. His great preoccupation is to complete his job before his sun has set. If there is beauty in sunlit dancing waters and the purple shadows of eventide on land and sea, if there is beauty in the written word, beauty in the angel faces that smile from the canvases of Titian and Giorgione it does not stir the soul of the senior Senator from Utah. Beauty is non-existent if it does not exist in the eye of the beholder. When Mr. Smoot journeyed to Europe to assist in the debt settlement we have no record of his impressions of the Winged Victory of Samothrace or the canvases of Botticelli, but we do have a record of his intense interest in the public finance and the bargaining tariffs of the several European States. Well, we can't all be dilettantes, art connoisseurs, box holders at symphony concerts, and murmurers of drawing-room graciocities and insipidities.

Men craving the stark truth of things can't be fed with rhetoric, metaphors, formulas. Senator Smoot's passion to know about things has saved the Treasury of the United States a great many million dollars. For twenty-five years he has waged war against the printing of piffle in the *Congressional Record*. Each printed page costs, I believe, sixty dollars. Waste of government money pains him acutely. Waste of anything affects him disagreeably like the presence of a civet-cat or a strong infusion of mustard gas.

The United States Bureau of Efficiency is the creation of Senator Smoot. This particular Bureau, one of forty-seven different varieties in Washington, is the official censor of extravagance and waste. It stands between the United States Treasury and a horde of high- and low-degree governmental wasters—wasters of time, money, equipment. It is easy to spend—hard to save. Easy to denounce extravagance in the abstract but hard to disoblige a friend in the concrete. It's difficult for men in authority to disappoint the little circle of importunate friends whom they continually see for the sake of saving a few pennies for the millions of unheard people whom they never see.

Democracy achieves the difficult task of government by the unscientific process of trial and error. Science is systematized knowledge. To be able to assemble the facts and draw correct deductions from them is all the difference between astronomy calculating the parallax of a fixed star and the Hagerstown almanac predicting in its January edition the state of the weather on next Michaelmas Day. Our legislators in such a weighty matter as tariff revision are becoming more judges than lawmakers. They act after hearing a vast mass of evidence on both sides. The old copy-book maxim, "Knowledge is power," still stands. As a pursuer and assembler of facts Senator Smoot has no peer in the present Congress. References have been made to his passion for saving. No less strong is his passion for statistics. An error in figures riles the Senator like the sibilant sound of a punctured motor tire when speeding to catch a train. If some one rises on the floor of the Senate and misquotes the import figures even of relatively unimportant commodities such as pichurim beans, Tasmanian stinkwood, broomstraw, truffles, wormgut, a zaffer, Mr. Smoot is upon the offender like a hawk on a jay-bird. The stream must be kept pure at its source. In the Smootian philosophy statistics form the groundwork of all sound legislation. Statistics bear the same relation to the science of practical government that chart and compass bear to the science of practical navigation. Nothing escapes the vigilance of Senator Smoot. He's at his office by eight o'clock in the morning, in his seat when the Senate Chaplain offers prayer, and if the session should last throughout the day and far into the night he's always there to complete a quorum. If a lull occurs about midday he allows himself ten minutes in the cloak-room for a bit of a sandwich and a glass of milk. The session over he seeks relaxation at home by analyzing the figures in the latest Statistical Abstract of the Department of Commerce. He thus finds relaxation out of working hours by working. Having drawn a cordon about himself he has learned to live comfortably with himself and that's more than some of the rest of us have learned.

The present tariff act bears his name, along with that of Representative Hawley of the House. Those who look for a monument in St. Paul's Cathedral to Sir Christopher Wren who built it are asked to look around them. The tariff act whatever its merits or demerits is a monumental piece of work. Witnesses to the number of 1,131 were heard by the Ways and Means Committee and 1,232 by the Senate Finance Committee. It took 11,000 closely printed pages to contain the information and argument submitted by interested parties. Data furnished by the Tariff Commission on all schedules fill two big volumes with a total of 2,750 printed pages. Debates ran to 2,800 pages

in the *Congressional Record.* In the fourteen
months consumed in preparation of the bill Mr.
Smoot lost thirty-five pounds in weight, but he
never missed a hearing in the Finance Committee
nor was he absent from his seat in the Senate when
any tariff item was under consideration. The
*Record* is punctuated on nearly every page with
inquiries addressed to Mr. Smoot during the running fire debates. Ask him a question and he re-
sponds with the gravity and exactitude of a precision instrument, and with as little humor. He's
a fine figure of a man and a magnificent man of
figures when he rises to his full height of six feet
two inches in his stocking feet (the chances are
that the stockings are of Utah wool protected under
the Tariff Act by a duty of thirty-four cents per
pound), and calls the turn on some luckless col-
league whose figures may happen to be either inadequate or erroneous, or both. In such moments
he lives up to his name. The old English verb "to
smite" goes—smitan, smōt, smitan. The form
"smoot" is not found in any Germanic tongue but
English which goes to show that Senator Smoot is
one hundred per cent. Anglo-Saxon.

During the debate on the milling in bond privilege enjoyed by Canadian wheat a usually well-
informed Senator observed that the amount of

flour so milled was relatively unimportant, whereupon Senator Smoot mildly interjected the precise information that the city of Buffalo alone produced nine million barrels of flour annually of which four million five hundred thousand barrels were ground from Canadian wheat.

When one of the Senators asked for a duty on citron for the sake of protecting the free market for Porto Rican citron in the United States Senator Smoot dryly remarked that not a single pound of Porto Rican citron comes into the United States.

When another Senator insisted that the duty on mustard-seed should be reduced because our production of this commodity is negligible Senator Smoot offhand submitted figures on our mustard-seed crop for the past twenty years, pointing out that the state of California alone has produced as much as four million pounds of mustard-seed in a single year.

With the tariff debate running along smoothly, nothing contentious, not a cloud in the sky, faith at the zenith, the Senate was thrown into an uproar by the proposition to place a higher duty upon fresh beans. Senator Walsh, of Massachusetts, rushed to the defense of the Boston baked-bean industry. "I implore the Senate," he supplicated, "to be charitable and let us have our baked beans at a little lower price." Other Senators defended the sacred rights of the particular beans indigenous to their localities. The Lima bean, the string-bean, the snap-bean, the navy-bean, the fordhook bean all had their day in court praying to be defended from the aggression of the Mexican jumping bean and all other intrusive beans of whatever variety from foreign parts whenever and wherever grown to the detriment of the peace, dignity and security of beans grown on the soil of the good old U. S. A. The bean controversy sputtered through many pages of the *Congressional Record* until Senator Smoot, rising gaunt and gray, like Father Neptune above the stormy waters, spoke to this effect: "Why all this fuss? The item under consideration deals only with fresh winter string-beans grown in semi-tropical countries. The first shipment of foreign green beans came into this country on the seventh of November last with the final shipment arriving on the thirteenth day of February. Not a foreign string-bean from any place on earth comes into this country except in the winter months, when green beans are not produced domestically." The last word on beans!

Occasionally Jove nods. When the duty on infants' hosiery was under consideration Senator Harrison questioned Mr. Smoot's accuracy in classifying eight-inch hosiery as wear for infants. "Doesn't an infant," he inquired, "with feet eight inches long cease to be an infant?"

"Eight inches," vouchsafed Senator Smoot severely, "means a sock with a four-inch foot plus a four-inch leg. That's all there is to it."

No, not quite all, because the trade invariably classifies the size of hosiery by the number of inches measured from tip of heel to tip of toe.

As Chairman of the Senate Finance Committee and ranking member of the Committee on Appropriations Senator Smoot's all-seeing eye, like that of Providence itself, watches over the tens of thousands of items which enter into the national income and outgo. Figure over your modest income tax items and try to grasp, if you please, the intricacies and complexities of a day-book and ledger account of the national income and outgo of one hundred and twenty million people. The job is almost beyond human comprehension. As the tariff is one of the dullest subjects in the world, so public finance is one of the most complicated. Thus it is that Senator Smoot wallows gloriously and triumphantly in one of the dullest and most complicated messes that have taxed the human understanding since this ordered universe emerged from primordial chaos.

A wretched prisoner in the days of the Medici, so the story goes, was given his choice between indefinite imprisonment and the perusal of Guicciardini's *History of the Pisan-Florentine Wars.* After looking into the heavy tomes he asked to be remanded to his dungeon. Let some modern Guicciardini write a conscientious commentary on the morphology and processes of the administration of the Federal Government. Put government to the laboratory test; see what the microscope has to reveal as to its functions and processes. Subject the human factors in the equation to efficiency's test tube. It's like a study of the cosmic process itself. Where will you begin? Where will you leave off? Congress enacts laws. They are not drawn out of the air nor do statutes administer themselves. The work is performed by thousands of persons—swarming, incessant human beings— by men with big jobs and big responsibilities and by little men busily important about unimportant things. Functionaries who see that the fishes are put to bed, that the lights are lit along our coasts at night, that grizzly bears are protected in one part of the country and pocket gophers pursued in another. Savants who treat of domestic fowls and their parasites; others who advise as to the art of crating goods for export, others who reveal the secret of iridescence in fish scales. Men who make rules, others who interpret them, others who enforce them. Thousands of buck-passers, chairwarmers, clock-watchers. Officialdom with its little jealousies, petty professionalisms, ponderous protected ignorance. Red tape with the formulas, traditions, formalisms dear to the heart of all true bureaucrats. Beneath all these wrappages and incrustations, youthful enthusiasms and mental resiliences become extinct along with graying hair and progressive hardening of the arteries.

Towering above the great mass of petty officials stands Senator Smoot, a titan among pigmies. Now, Master, after so many years of labor pray take a little rest. Not he—

"Back to his studies, fresher than at first,
    Fierce as a dragon
He (soul hydroptic with a sacred thirst)
    Sucked at the flagon."

Over the career of Senator Smoot hovers a vast interrogation. Why is he what he is? What pleasure does he find in statistics? What fun does he get out of life? Why not saunter outdoors in the sunshine, play a little golf? Once upon a time this notion did occur to him but his bag of golf sticks stands in a corner covered with dust like the toys of Little Boy Blue.

In times past Mr. Smoot diverted himself by an occasional visit to the Washington zoo. One morning he and Mrs. Coolidge met by appointment at eight o'clock to witness how a litter of bear cubs behaves on the forty-second day after birth when they first open their eyes upon this sinful world. It was in the Washington zoo that he cultivated the friendship of a pretty parrot named Helen. Helen would poke her head through the bars and mildly bite in affectionate playfulness the long bony finger of her tall admirer from Utah. Helen would also proffer her head to be scratched. But things took a bad turn one day when Mr. Smoot coaxingly demanded, "Now come, Helen, give me a little kiss." Whereupon the capricious bird backed away, ruffled up her neck feathers, and screamed, "No, no, no, you go to hell!" Mr. Smoot moved wearily and mournfully away and was not seen again in those parts. The flouting of the gentleman from Utah by pretty Helen can not be accepted as one of those etiological myths that cling to great personalities—such as the legendary rebuke of King Alfred the Great by the neatherd's wife. The writer received the information from the Senator's own lips. It's a matter of history, too, that Mr. Smoot got a fat appropriation through Congress for the construction of a magnificent bird

Senator Smoot at his desk

house at the zoo during the period when he and Helen were in cahoots. A suburban neighbor of the Senator owns a pet chimpanzee which eats bananas with a knife and fork. One day, confronted by Senator Smoot, who was invited over to witness the performance, the intelligent chimpanzee dropped the knife and fork, threw away the banana, and placed its arms affectionately around the neck of Mr. Smoot. A just recognition, let us believe, of the Senator's efforts to block the proposed insensate import duty on bananas.

Mr. Smoot has been known to attend the theater and gaze mournfully and inquiringly at the comedian when he springs a jest that convulses the rest of the audience. Humor is not one of his strong points. When the tariff on toys was under discussion a big table on the Republican side of the Senate was loaded with toys, one of which was a miniature band-wagon imported from Germany. These exhibits were presided over by Senator Smoot. When he wasn't looking some wag hung a sign on the band-wagon reading "Boy Scouts," an appellation given to a certain group of younger statesmen with aspirations for leadership. Some one asked the Senator if he had attached the Boy-Scouts label to the band-wagon. "I certainly did not," rasped the Apostle of the Mormon Church, seeing no humor in the implication. No, life is a serious business, particularly to the contemplative person approaching the allotted threescore years and ten. Senator Smoot in his sixty-ninth year finds no time for frittering and fribbling.

"We are all under sentence of death," writes Victor Hugo, "but with a sort of indefinite reprieve. We have our interval and our place knows us no more forever." Walter Pater, asking how mortals should best spend this interval—this short day of frost and sun before evening, concludes that the wisest of the children of this world will spend their interval in art and song. Well, Senator Smoot's art is the application of statistics to the affairs of government. Few men who have accomplished much in the world bother themselves about assessing the measure of their success. When it comes to measuring such abstract concepts as success or happiness there is no measure. As well ask, how long is long? We do know this, that man, like certain of the lower organisms, is goaded by an instinct for work, for struggle. Why do men forsake the soft way for the hard way? Why do we struggle up-stream against the current? We only know that men following the larval instinct crawl out of circumscribed wrappages of poverty and obscurity and struggle upward toward the light.

Certain philosophers and theologians have been able to detect amid all the helter-skelter of the universe traces of order, purpose, design. So in the vast conglomeration of governmental functions it is reassuring to feel that things are not running haphazard and at loose ends but are presided over by intelligence and unity of purpose. It is good to reflect that somebody knows what it is all about and can supply the key to endless enigmas. What does the following paragraph in the tariff act refer to:

"Cotton cloth, printed, dyed, colored, unwoven, figured, not containing silk or artificial silk, forty per cent. or more colored with vat dyes with an average count not exceeding number twenty-four."

Senator Smoot will tell you that it refers to striped bed ticking, though the article is not mentioned by name in the paragraph.

Again, in reading over the coal-tar paragraphs one might not know offhand the difference between dimethylphenylbenzylammonium and tetramethyldiaminodiphenylmethane. But Senator Smoot knows.

"The Ball no Questions asks of Ayes or Noes,
But Here or There as strikes the Player, goes;
   And He that toss'd you down into the Field,
*He* knows about it all—HE knows, HE knows!"

[ 223 ]

Finally, work and religion with Senator Smoot are correlative terms. According to the Mormon faith death does not end all. This brief life is but the prelude to a more highly developed life beyond. According to the teachings of the Mormon Apostles whatever principles of intelligence we attain to in this life will rise with us in the resurrection and any man who by his greater diligence and understanding acquires more knowledge than another will have just that much advantage in the world to come. It is impossible for men to be saved in ignorance. Perhaps that is one reason why Utah ranks among the leading states of the Union educationally, and why Mr. Smoot plugs away at statistics with almost fanatical fervor. Maybe he's just made that way, just as an ostrich is made to gobble up glass beads and persimmon seeds.

Senator Smoot will tell you that since he is moderate in everything else he can afford to be immoderate in work. His shoes never squeak, he never laughs aloud, never perspires, never cusses (beyond the intensives strictly permissible in diaconal and apostolic speech), does not smoke or chew tobacco or drink anything stronger than ginger pop and sarsaparilla. In arts of expression he believes with Edmund Burke in the strength of moderation, or what Jeremy Taylor calls "the prudent endearment of moderate speech." When it comes to the tariff he's a protectionist beyond cavil. "I am not a spotted protectionist," he declares, "I am a protectionist all the way through." Just the same it's well known that Senator Smoot during the debates in the Finance Committee monotonously voted for moderate rather than extreme duties. Sheep and sugar are the objects of his passionate solicitude. The original Mormon settlers in Utah were first of all herdsmen. In the rude economy of shepherds' lives they learned what there is to know about mutton as a food and wool as a covering for the human body. The energetic Sir John Sinclair danced one evening in a suit of woolen broadcloth which the day before had been growing as wool on the back of a sheep. Senator Smoot has forgotten more about wool and woolens than Sir John ever knew. After twenty-seven years in the Senate he can draw up in the minutest detail specifications for an up-to-date wool spinning and weaving mill and operate the mill when set up.

The sugar-beet thrives well in Utah when properly tilled and irrigated. Senator Smoot's father imported from Europe the first sugar mill west of the Rocky Mountains. Thus Utah has two agricultural strings to her bow—sheep and sugar. Senator Smoot would have been less than human if he had not pressed for increases in the duties on wool and sugar. But the increases he asked and got in the present tariff act are moderate increases—an extra three cents per pound on wool and an extra quarter of a cent a pound on raw sugar.

Walter Bagehot sets down "animated moderation" as the winning quality in politics. Strongly idiosyncratic minds violently disposed to extremes of opinion are soon weeded out of American politics.

Senator Smoot looks tired—he is tired. He bears the look of an aging man who became tired shortly after birth and has remained tired ever since. He has few intimates. He lives in a big white house set down in a grove of trees some seven miles from Capitol Hill. And judging from the number of bird-houses the Senator has set up in his back yard he qualifies for all the Audubon Societies in America.

Mr. Smoot finds delightful companionship in his first great-grandchild. He makes big eyes and shakes a bony finger at this bit of humanity. The wide-open eyes of the baby staring forth in blank wonderment at the universe meet tired wise eyes that look back across the chasm of the hurrying years. But they seem to understand and admire each other. The solemn face of the Apostle (with but two lives intervening between Apostleship and Headship of the Mormon Church) is lit by a smile—a smile like a ray of sun gleaming through clouds on an Arctic landscape.   A touch of spring after a long hard winter.   Age brings compensations and finds one somehow or other pathetically content.   A world with plenty of toil and trouble, but not a bad world, after all, to live in.

# CHAPTER VII

## Dr. Ivan Bratt and European Prohibition Experiments

For the space of six years on end the writer represented the United States Department of Commerce on various missions in some fifteen European countries. Observing different people drinking alcohol in different fashion and with different effects he came to be deeply interested in the drink question.

I have no pet theory to expound, no program to advocate, no ism to popularize. I find both the taste and effects of alcohol disagreeable. Nature made me a poor reveler. Where others are exhilarated and emancipated by alcohol I suffer an access of depressing stupidity with plenty of headache to follow. That men find pleasure in strong drink is a marvel and a mystery to me. This angle of the drink question was the first to challenge my thought. It was this unanswered interrogation that led me into the inquiry which I am just now setting down on paper.

Whether freedom to drink as one pleases is a good thing or a bad thing depends upon whether one's point of view is that of an ethical teacher, a humanitarian, a utilitarian philosopher, or finally, the type of liberal who believes that an individual should be perfectly free to go to the devil by whatever route he may fancy.

One may turn with interest from baffling impressions as to the success of prohibition in the United States to recent European experiments in liquor control. Norway has given up limited prohibition for high license. Russia has abandoned prohibition and returned to vodka. Finland and the United States are the only important laboratories in which the experiment of prohibition is being conducted on a nation-wide scale. Sweden is in a class by itself. The prohibition issue no longer exists in Sweden. In lieu thereof a control system has been set up that is unique among legislative attempts to deal with the liquor problem. It is rather startling to the imagination to find one country on the face of the globe where the extreme wets and extreme drys no longer fill the world with their clamor and fury.

I shall use Doctor Bratt as a convenient trellis upon which to drape an otherwise fragmentary and disconnected narrative. Doctor Bratt has given his name to the Swedish system of liquor control. For aught I know his name is like to outlive that of Julius Cæsar. There's nothing reticent about Doctor Bratt when he comes to appraise the sanity and soundness of the program which he modestly designates as the Stockholm System. Like the tactful politician intent upon riding his hobby he uses the plural personal pronoun "we" instead of "I" when recounting his achievements. Doctor Bratt is a profuse sayer of words and doer of things; that is to say he combines the man of talk with the man of action.

In the literal etymological sense he takes himself to be a soothsayer when it comes to words about the use and abuse of alcohol. He harangues his fellow citizens in incisive convincing Swedish and will switch in an argument as occasion demands to perfect German, French or English. In appearance Doctor Bratt suggests the cleric turned college professor—clean shaven, bespectacled, intellectually peering, curious, eager like the Athenians to hear something new and piquant. But all conversational roads lead to the Rome of liquor control. Doctor Bratt was graduated from the ancient University of Upsala in the Class of 1903, along with Excellency Bostrom, Sweden's delightful Minister to the United States. Verging on fifty he's given about half of his workaday life to the solution of the liquor question. The Swedes have been among the world's more important drinkers ever since the pagan warriors of the antique world celebrated their victories by the good old custom of quaffing mead from the skulls of their enemies. *Skoal* is about the first Scandinavian word that a visiting stranger picks up in contact with convivial, warm-hearted Swedes.

In his earlier years Doctor Bratt was attending physician in a Stockholm hospital and learned from daily observation what too much alcohol does for a man. To his mind the essence of the drink evil does not lie in the average per capita amount consumed in Sweden but in the excess amount consumed by persons to whom liquor proves a curse.

The extreme drys contend that alcohol is detrimental to all users. Doctor Bratt, physiologist and skilled medical practitioner, does not accept this view; nor does he believe in prohibition. He sees no justice in penalizing all users of liquor because a few consumers drink to excess. Doctor Bratt is neither a wet nor a dry. For years he was intensely disliked by the extreme drys who looked upon him as an *advocatus diaboli* in favoring the moderate use of alcohol. He was just as much disliked by the extreme wets who regarded him as a conspir-

[ 231 ]

ator against the natural and inalienable right of every man to booze according to his notion. When Doctor Bratt started his national campaign some fifteen or more years ago he acted on the assumption that prohibition is just as much a social evil as free and unlimited drink. In the thought of Doctor Bratt prohibition as a short-cut settlement of the liquor problem was entirely too simple. Human nature, he maintains, controls the key to the liquor question. It is not only the stomach that demands liquor but the head as well. The stomach may be indifferent to liquor but the head, craving self-determination, will not be denied independence of action. As a proposition in human nature he could not contemplate a program of national prohibition without the inevitable sequences of smuggling, home-brewing, bootlegging, racketeering. The two great evils of drink, in his philosophy, were abuse by certain persons of the use of alcohol and the profiteering in its manufacture and sale.

In Sweden the natives don't mind admitting that they have the best system of liquor-control in the world. Under the Bratt system the liquor business in Sweden has been taken out of private hands and vested in disinterested management. Drink is sold on the passport principle. Unless a man possesses a *motbok,* or pass book, he can not legally purchase a bottle of schnapps or vodka in Sweden. To secure a *motbok* requires more formalities than obtaining a passport in the United States. The claims of the applicant are subjected to rigid scrutiny. He must be an orderly, decent, deserving fellow. Deserving women may obtain *motboks,* but if a married woman is fortunate enough to obtain one *motbok,* her husband can not. In the Swedish restaurants drinking is associated with the purchase of food. The amount of drink is strictly limited. As, for example, in the case of schnapps to a glass and a half. The government must know to whom the restaurants sell, how much they sell, and when they sell. In the case of spirits sold by the bottle or gallon, no transaction takes place except on a *motbok* basis, and a *motbok* when once issued is good but for one specified vending place. Beer is exempt from *motbok* control under the Bratt system, but it is illegal to manufacture beer stronger than four per cent.

In Sweden the government exercises an all-seeing, paternalistic care as to who shall drink, where he shall drink and how much he shall drink. Doctor Bratt informed the writer that the consumption of spirits had decreased fifty per cent. in Stockholm since the inauguration of the system which bears his name. Street arrests for drunkenness have decreased sixty per cent., hospital cases of chronic alcoholism seventy per cent. There are no slums and no extreme poverty in the city of Stockholm. The saloon has become extinct in Sweden and the bootlegger has ceased to ply his trade.

The essence of the Bratt System is this: All wines and spirits containing over three and six-tenths per cent. alcohol are handled through a single hand— the Wine and Spirits Central Control. This central organization distributes to one hundred twenty local concerns throughout the kingdom. The local distributors provide a *motbok* which entitles the owner to four liters of spirits a month. In public places drink is served to all comers but the amount of spirits is based on the amount of food consumed, with a fixed maximum quantity permitted within the day's selling hours. All profits that accrue to the Wine and Spirits Central above five per cent. go to the government. All financial incentive is thus taken out of the liquor traffic. The Bratt system, after fourteen years of trial, has passed beyond the experimental stage and is accepted by the Swedish population as a permanent settlement of the liquor problem.

Now as to European countries where nation-wide prohibition has been attempted: One must take account of the commonplace truth that the human reaction to alcohol is infinitely varied. What is one man's meat is another man's poison. Alcohol exerts different effects upon the same individual at different times and under different conditions of health. From the standpoint of social injury a per capita consumption of two liters of alcohol a year in Norway or Finland may be more destructive than a consumption of fifteen to eighteen liters in Spain and Italy. It depends upon whether alcohol is sipped or gulped; whether it is taken highly diluted in wine or beer, or highly concentrated in vodka and schnapps; whether it is gulped down on an empty stomach, as is the custom in vodka-drinking countries, or whether it is sipped in cafés in conjunction with food, as is the custom in wine- and beer-drinking countries.

When it comes to national temperament and race psychology, the effects of drink are one thing in France, another in Finland, another in England, another in Germany and quite another in Russia. Where the French or Italian wine-bibber is stimulated to agreeable conversation by drink, or where the Englishman in drink becomes red-eyed, sleepy and buttoned-up, or where the vodka-drinking Finn displays an ugly temper and concludes his argument by reaching for an inimical dirk, the Russian in his cups relapses into introspective sadness or interminable argument. What pleasurable reaction does the Russian derive from gulping down his brandy? Is he sad because he drinks, or does he drink because he is sad? These considerations are not always perfectly understood by our visitors to European countries.

The per capita consumption of alcohol in France is extremely high but a visitor may tarry for weeks in Paris and witness less drunkenness than he would observe in the city of Washington. The French and Germans take their drink slowly—drinkers who sit and sip rather than drinkers who stand and gulp.

It makes a vast difference when it comes to social injury. Roughly speaking the per capita consumption of alcohol in the northern European countries, while far less than in the wine-producing countries to the south, is relatively more destructive. In Italy, for example, wine is drunk as freely as water. In some localities, such as Rimini, wine almost entirely supplants water as a beverage. The evil effects of drink are associated not with drinking in the home or in restaurants but in the *trattorie* or saloons. Mussolini's idea is not to get rid of drink but to get rid of the degrading influences which attach to the saloon.

Vodka is sold in Russia to-day as freely as ice-cream is sold in the United States. This pale volatile stuff is forty per cent. pure alcohol and three stiff glasses of it are enough to put any novice under the table. Russia tried out prohibition for the space of ten years and in 1925 definitely abandoned it. Drinking in Russia is not the kind we know. For the most part a man drinks standing rather than sitting and gulps his liquor rather than sips it. Taste runs to fiery potent liquors rather than to wine and beer. The Russian drinks not for sociability and companionship, but primarily to get drunk. These Russians can drink too. Only a superman at carrying his liquor may hope in Russia to attain distinction as a drinker.

The production of vodka in Russia is associated with the ordinary potato. Stuff powerful enough to blister the paint from a barn door is distilled from the watery and anemic potato. From one peck of potatoes may be extracted enough alcohol to liven up any household wedding or christening. Let us begin this tale, after a manner of speaking, from the ground up—that is, with the potato.

Russia before the war knew no rival as a potato country. Wherever the potato thrives in eastern Europe, there vodka flourishes. The most favored potato regions in old Russia were the western marches of the country. Esthonia, Latvia, Congress Poland—territories now independent of Russia—annually produced from one thousand five hundred to two thousand pounds of potatoes per capita, while the production in our own country scarcely averages two hundred pounds.

The diminutive republic of Esthonia, as a part of Russia, specialized before the war in potatoes and vodka. It supplied Russia annually with about ten million gallons of alcohol. About one million gallons were consumed locally in this sparsely settled country about the area of West Virginia. In the pre-war period the Esthonian peasant partook of a light breakfast of potato bread and alcohol. At noon his luncheon consisted of a snack of dried fish and a snifter of vodka. Shortly thereafter he knocked off for the day.

This concentration on vodka created no international trade balance. Esthonia, as a Russian province, was a poor country with a limited future. As an independent republic, with the Russian vodka market lost and its production cut ninety-per cent., Esthonia to-day is one of the few countries in Europe that balances its budget and maintains a favorable international trade balance. Esthonia is growing just as many potatoes—some one thousand five hundred pounds per capita—but the spud crop is being fed to animals and converted into milk and butter instead of alcohol. The little republic within ten years has waxed consequential as a dairy country, with exports of butter, bacon and lard exceeding the value of the pre-war vodka trade. The Russians patronizingly refer to Esthonia as the little potato republic.

Before the war, the Russian potato-alcohol industry was concentrated in Congress Poland, that of Germany in the Posen territory and that of Austria in Galicia. Congress Poland, Posen and Galicia now combine to form Poland. Consequently Poland is overburdened with an excessive alcohol output which it can not dispose of to foreign consumers because of the universally high tariffs upon spirits, whereas Russia, Austria and Germany are short of an important article of commerce formerly produced within their own borders.

One drives over the great estates of Poland and observes the country dotted with potato distilleries. Poland is glutted with potato alcohol while neighboring countries are short of it. Sweden, with its strict licensing system, and Finland, on a prohibition basis, both complain of the quantities of potato alcohol that are smuggled in from Poland.

The return of Russia, in 1925, to the vodka traffic found the country short of supplies and under the necessity of developing the domestic sources of production. The Russians have been rather slow to resume their old drinking habits, because it has taken time to build up production within the Soviet union. The alcohol trade of Russia before the war was a government monopoly. Under the czarist régime the drinker obtained his bottle of government alcohol in exchange for a few kopecks. With one movement he knocked the stopper out of the bottle by striking its bottom against the palm of his hand, gulped down the contents and restored the empty bottle to the vender, receiving a copper or two in exchange. By adding a few more kopecks he could acquire another bottle and so keep on drinking in a perpendicular position until his money was exhausted or he sank stupefied to the ground. Vodka-drinking would have dealt a severe blow to agriculture but for the fact that much of the farm work is done by women, and Russian women are not inebriates.

Turgenef, the most faithful of Russian realists, writes of the drinking in Russian villages of his day:

"Before almost every dramshop were standing little peasant carts, harnessed to shaggy, pot-bellied nags which stood with their unkempt heads hanging down submissively and seemed to sleep. From doors in the huts coarse voices broke forth, from doors suddenly opened streamed the filthy warmth and acrid smell of alcohol and the red glare of lights. A ragged unbelted peasant would come out of a dramshop and, his breast propped against the shafts of his cart, stay motionless, feebly fumbling and moving his hands as though looking for something; or a wretched factory hand, his cap awry and his cotton shirt flying open, would take a few irresolute steps barefoot, stop short, scratch his spine, and with a sudden groan go back again."

The average Russian vodka seller was more of a social and political menace than the American saloon-keeper at his worst. The Russian publican was more than a dramshop keeper. He was all too frequently money-lender and usurer. When a patron fell hopelessly into debt, the vodka seller would exact the debtor's labor. Both laborers and peasants became bondmen to the drink seller.

Count Witte, most capable of modern Russian statesmen, recognized these evils and, along with Bismarck, was quick to see the revenue-raising possibilities of a state-liquor monopoly. Witte also stressed the humanitarian side of putting the government into the drink business. The evils of drink, he argued, are directly associated with the poisonousness of impure alcohol. He pointed out that better refining methods are assured under a state monopoly, and that many of the evils of drunkenness would disappear if the state were in a position to guarantee the purity of alcoholic beverages. He argued that a state monopoly enabled the government to fight alcoholism, and with this argument won over Emperor Alexander in spite of the opposition of Pobyedonostsev, chief of the Holy Synod.

When the control of all retail dramshops was taken over by the state not less than one hundred thousand vodka saloons were closed. The clergy blessed the new government shops, and certain be-medaled aristocrats graced the auspicious occasion by acting as bartenders. The government began in a spirit of moderation. In the first year consumption of government vodka amounted to no more than forty-four million gallons. But soon thereafter the Japanese War broke out. As William Pitt had found in the elasticity of the British spirits duty a convenient source of revenue for carrying on Continental wars, so Russia, in the crucial struggle with Japan, turned to vodka as a means for liquidating the enormous expense of the war.

Within fifteen years after setting up the state vodka monopoly consumption rose from forty-four million to two hundred fifty million gallons. The state came to draw an annual revenue of five hundred million dollars from the vodka monopoly.

Thus Witte's state vodka monopoly, having begun with the purest protestations and the highest hopes, plunged the country in the liquor business up to the hilt. The aim was no longer to restrict but to increase the consumption of vodka. No police measures were taken against drunkenness and the number of dramshops doubled.

When the World War broke out prohibition was decreed for Russia by the Czar with as little ceremony or agitation as a change in a railroad timetable. It was done in a flash as a war measure—first, because the sober Russian is a better fighter than a drunken one; second, because of the necessity for conserving grain. With the Czar's edict dramshops were closed, stocks destroyed, distilleries dismantled. The police, with their elaborate secret-service system, saw to it that the Czar's edict was respected. One day plenty of vodka, the next day a positive dearth. The will of the Czar was like an act of Providence against which the individual may recalcitrate in vain.

It didn't require highly concentrated power to decree prohibition for Russia, but it did take unlimited autocratic power to enforce it. The Russian autocracy was a despotism tempered only by assassination. The will of the Czar was supreme law.

The omnipotent Czar, with his omnipresent police, had to do with a people habituated to obedience and submissive under authority. Most Russians of the old days were bred to the belief that the world is divided into masters whose privilege it is to command and simple folk whose duty it is to obey. Under the Czar, prohibition prohibited.

As prohibition in Russia was dictated by military necessity, so the return to vodka was dictated by political expediency. After the fall of the Czarist régime the peasant turned home distiller and booze peddler. Back in 1919 the Soviet Government requisitioned the farmers' grain to feed the half-starved city workers. The hard-headed peasant, cold to the great communistic experiment, found no satisfaction in exchanging his grain, which could be eaten and possessed an intrinsic value, for pieces of paper called rubles which possessed a fluctuating and declining value.

The peasant responded to grain requisitioning by hiding his surplus grain in hollow trees or burying it in the ground. Village geniuses with a talent for discovering the obvious perceived that alcohol keeps better than grain, has a more universal marketing appeal and can be secreted and sold with greater facility. Home distillation and bootlegging spread like wildfire.

The Soviet Government found itself whipsawed by prohibition. It could neither suppress the contraband trade in vodka nor endure it. Home distilling at once wasted the grain the Soviet Government essentially needed as a medium of international exchange, and at the same time deprived the government of the revenues that might be derived from legalized trade in spirits. The Soviet in turn had to beat a retreat.

The business of saving the face was difficult. Trotzky had declared that prohibition was one of the iron assets of the revolution and would not be abandoned. History exactly repeated itself. Like Count Witte of earlier days, the Soviet sought to justify resumption of the vodka monopoly on broad humanitarian and financial grounds. If the people must drink, let them drink pure rather than poisonous liquor. If money was to be spent on drink, let the state treasury be the beneficiary rather than a horde of lawbreakers and bootleggers.

The Reverend Prokhonoff, president of the All-Russian Union of Evangelical Churches, is quoted as stating:

"Under prohibition, instead of having one drunkard in a Russian home, as was the case before prohibition was tried, every house became a distillery and a saloon. Men and women made vodka and even served it to their children."

Commissar of Public Health Semashko defends the return to vodka on the ground of public health. Since the Russians can not be prevented from making moonshine alcohol and drinking it, it is far better that they should have good stuff duly certified by the government than the poisonous bootleg stuff they were getting clandestinely.

Vodka may be had in the Russian cafés, or *tractirs* where food is served with drink. As in an American cafeteria, the café patron goes up to a buffet with his plate, selects a bit of raw fish or cucumber salad and returns to his table, where he is served with vodka as long as he can pay for it. Drinking in the Russian cafés has never been so destructive socially as drinking in the government shops. Here the drink is taken ordinarily without food, and drinking is associated with poverty. As between food and drink, the vodka addict chooses drink. On the whole, drinking in the government shops where the bottle is passed out and emptied at a gulp reflects the poverty and monotony of Russian middle-class life.

These men of dull unemotional lives appear to be reaching out pathetically for something to give spice to existence. These are the people who eat their heavy black bread sprinkled over with caraway seeds and their insipid raw cucumbers drowned in sour cream. Just here it may be observed that Riga is the world's true magnetic pole for caraway seeds. The people of Riga were the first, I believe, to originate the practise of mixing caraway seeds with food and drink. Pale, colorless vodka, blistering to the throat as turpentine, when infused with caraway seeds masquerades under the name of kümmel.

Lying east of Riga some five hundred miles is Nezhin, the center of the world's cucumber trade, embracing in its zone European Russia, the Baltic States and Congress Poland.

The Russians have a tepid national soft drink known as kvass, concocted from the fermented crusts of rye bread. When colored red, after the manner of circus lemonade, it is drunk with gusto as a cheap substitute for vodka. The Russian lumberjacks run their rafts down the Dwina River with a larder consisting of kvass, cucumbers and black bread. With this fare they are perfectly satisfied.

Striking likenesses and dissimilarities crop out in comparing the administration of the prohibition law in Finland and the United States. In both countries prohibition was ushered in as a war emergency, but long antecedent preparation had been going on. For some four or five decades temperance societies have been at work in Finland as in this country, and public opinion, particularly in the rural districts, had reached a point where it would support strict legislative limitations on the consumption of liquor. Finland, one is inclined to judge, was in a more advanced state of preparedness for prohibition than the United States.

The Finns are a highly disciplined people. For centuries they have been a subjugated race and, except for the Swedish element, are a homogeneous people. Racially they are Hungarian rather than Slavic. Their Russian conquerors have hardly left a chemical trace of Slavic influence. The besotted ignorance of the Russian peasant finds no counterpart in Finland. Illiterates are about as plentiful in Finland as albinos in the United States, and are as much out of their element as a Gila monster on Boston Common.

The Finns are the most omnivorous readers in Europe, and the public bookstore in Helsingfors is second to none on the Continent. The Finns, like the progressive Athenians of Paul's day, are the liberals of their epoch. To the Finn every new social experiment is worth a try-out. The Finns were the first of the Europeans to grant complete suffrage to women, and among the first of the war-distracted peoples to balance their budget and restore their international trade equilibrium. They were the first to boast the presence of a barefoot legislator on the floor of their national Parliament.

Finland is a country of strong men and strong liquors. They obey the Nietzschean theory, "Be strong and live." It is also a country of gray skies, cheerless landscapes, gloomy festivities. Nature has dealt with the land in niggard fashion, bestowing neither copper, coal, iron, petroleum, or any prime prerequisite of latter-day industrialism, with the exception of timber. For half the year darkness broods over the land for the better part of the working-day. In midsummer the sun rises shortly after two in the morning, and the flies at least a half-hour earlier. Characteristic of the national school of painting are canvases portraying struggles with forest fires, tempestuous seas, heroic efforts to subdue the wilderness. The favorite type of moving picture in Finland depicts physical struggle with wind and wave or human adversaries. The tragic Finn takes his pleasure sadly. He will sit through a film performance by Charlie Chaplin or Harold Lloyd and never crack a smile.

All this by way of explaining the fact that the

Finn is a grim determined fellow, who, having put his hand to a difficult job, such as prohibition, sees it through. The Czarist Government gave no support to the temperance movement in any part of the vast Russian domain. With the outbreak of the war, prohibition was decreed for Finland overnight by imperial edict. Prohibition, which came in like a flash, was amazingly effective at first because the Russian police power was behind it. When Finland threw off Russian overlordship some ten years ago, prohibition was continued by act of the Finnish Parliament.

The difficulties of administering the prohibition law in Finland, as in the United States, are partly physical and partly psychological. With respect to physical difficulties, the Finns have much more to contend with than we. With respect to psychology, about the same cleavages of public opinion obtain in both countries.

Finland is set down in the midst of an archipelago of ten thousand small islands. The country has a long coast-line to police, and this coast-line is deeply indented and fringed with a heavy forest cover. More ideal specifications for facilitating liquor-smuggling could not have been devised by the president of the bootleggers' union.

Excellency Venalainen, Director of Prohibition Enforcement, has no illusions about the difficulty

Dr. Ivan Bratt

Now that the government makes vodka. Nash Mir (Berlin)

Workers of world unite—at the saloon. Rul (Berlin)

of his job. He told the writer that his country was unable to bear the financial burden of adequately enforcing the law. "We can make no pretense of enforcing the law with the limited means now at our disposal. We inconvenience the rum-runners—we do not frustrate them."

In other words, enforcement could be had at a price, but the Finns lack the price. Their present resources are pitifully inadequate.

Enforcement of any law is at bottom a matter of public opinion. In Finland, as in the United States, public opinion is mixed.

In Finland urban virtuosos of bibulosity proclaim that prohibition is a delusion and a snare. Most of the Finnish country folk have a good word to say for prohibition. "Under prohibition we can get liquor when we need it for a wedding or a christening, and we are jolly well rid of the odious saloon and disgusting drunkenness on the streets."

I remarked to a highly intelligent Finnish friend, who is perfectly rational on all subjects except prohibition, that in the space of a week I had not observed a single case of drunkenness in Finland. The assertion nettled him, touching some live, quivering nerve of patriotic emotion. He sprang to the defense of the good name and fame of his people as nullifiers of their prohibition law.

"You should have been with me last Saturday afternoon. In a hundred-and-fifty-mile drive from Abo to Helsingfors I ran into drunken brawls in every village. Booze as strong as concentrated lye was being served everywhere. If you want to see drunken Finns, don't look for them in the heart of the city. Visit by night the Brunns House on the edge of town and you will see how good fellows get together in Finland and drink themselves under the table."

I dropped into the designated de luxe restaurant that same evening, prepared to be shocked. Little groups here and there were partaking of the national dish—cucumbers and sour cream. Other groups were sipping wine and beer, and here and there a glass of pale colorless vodka was in process of being quaffed. By no stretch of the imagination could it be perceived that any of the patrons were the worse for liquor. The only altercation that occurred during the evening was between the writer and a waiter who insisted on substituting an invoice of pallid sliced cucumbers swimming in sour cream in lieu of the requested portion of ice-cream. The evening was as decorously dull as a dirge played on a hurdy-gurdy in a morgue on a rainy Sunday afternoon.

The next day I complained to my friend of the

barren quest. He was plainly vexed. "You took the wrong night for going out. You should have waited till Saturday night. If you want to see men perfectly drunk in shoals, Saturday night's the time. Our heavy boozers save up all week for a good souse on Saturday night, just as our people set aside the same evening for a steam-bath. But to test the thing out fairly, you should come around on Christmas or Saint John's Day and you will see Finns drunk by platoons."

As I had missed the annual feast of Saint John by only a fortnight and Christmas lay five months ahead, I was unable to complete the test.

A week later in Reval, Esthonia, where prohibition has long gone out, we dined in the mellow light of a fading summer's day at a concert-garden in the lovely Katarina Thal. Birds were twittering sleepily in the boughs overhead. The still air was heavy with the scent of fresh-cut hay. It turned out to be one of those scenes where every prospect pleases and only man is vile.

At an adjoining table sat a family group composed of father, mother, two sons in their early twenties, a daughter and a daughter-in-law. The family were dining conventionally on a snack of fish and a snifter of vodka. A family discussion broke out with protests, remonstrances, entreaties.

The occasion was a quart bottle of vodka which the men had insisted upon ordering against the protests of the mother, who now sat in dull misery with tears glistening on her faded cheeks as the men gulped down glass after glass of the fiery liquor, alternating with huge steins of beer. The young women had nothing to say, but occasionally one of them would lean over and give the troubled mother a reassuring pat on the arm. In twenty minutes the red-faced, perspiring men were gibbering and slobbering and snouting in their plates for food like swine. I have seen mothers leave their little children out on the sidewalk while they stupefied themselves with whisky in the pubs of London and Glasgow, but the spectacle was less revolting than these three drunken men sprawled about a public table in the presence of a weeping mother.

After the stupefied men had been bundled into droshkies by robust waiters and ignominiously hauled away, I inquired as to the identity of the crapulous heroes.

"Why, who but Finns?" replied the waiter with a contemptuous lift of the shoulders.

Ten years ago the per capita consumption of alcohol in Finland was the lowest in Europe, not exceeding a quart a year per person, or about one-twentieth the alcohol consumption of France, where prohibition has never become a national issue. The bulk of the Finnish population is temperate by education and habit, but the Finns who drink heavily are relatively more of a social menace than the inebriates of other European countries. It is an error to estimate the damage reflexes of alcohol by the amount consumed, just as it is a truism to state that alcohol affects different peoples in different ways, and even the same person in varying degrees of health.

Peoples of immoderate alcohol consumption, such as the Spaniards, the French, and the Italians, drink principally for purposes of stimulation, but associated with the ritual of drinking are ideas of relaxation, companionship, human cheer.

The Finn drinks not for sociability but to get drunk, and goes about it in a workmanlike fashion. He gulps his liquor and gulps it strong, and, like the Russian peasant drinking from the bottle in a government vodka shop, ordinarily drinks perpendicularly and on an empty stomach. Now a drunken Finn is a cultured Finn less his cultural inhibitions. In his cups he becomes the Ishmaelitish, warring, primitive man, the avenger of nameless oppressions.

It's not always fair weather when good Finns get together with a vodka bottle on the table. In fact, the chances are for foul weather. The drunken Finn, like Lucian the Roman satirist, possesses a cutting dialectic all his own. With a finish attributed to the Finnish, the Finn cleverly finishes an argument by lunging at his opponent with an inimical jack-knife.

If a drunken row breaks out in the low quarter of Copenhagen, the Danes with a shrug of their shoulders comment: "Those rascally drunken Swedes are at it again." If a drunken row breaks out in the old quarter of Stockholm, the Swedes set the matter down to "those terrible Finns." There is beauty neither in Finnish drinking-bouts nor in the eye of the beholder. The Finn after a half-liter of schnapps has about as much poise and self-control as a wren. While hard liquor may create in the Anglo-Saxon heart a love for all mankind, it turns the Finn sour and misanthropic. For the average man, the world seems a better place to live in after a good stiff drink. In the case of the Finn, the outlook grows darker as the bottle becomes lighter.

The Finnish Director of Prohibition Enforcement estimates that the police seize about one-tenth of the smuggled foreign liquor. Last year's seizures were estimated at seven hundred thousand liters of ninety-six per cent. alcohol. Ten times this amount is about two liters of alcohol for every living soul in the Finnish population, or double the amount consumed in the pre-prohibition era. If this estimate, which is checked by the captain of the rum-chasing flotilla, is correct, it is clear that England, Denmark and Sweden have discovered more effective methods of reducing alcohol consumption. In Denmark the price of spirits is about twelve times as high, and in England five or six times as high, as before the war. Largely because of the increased cost, the consumption of spirits in Denmark and England has fallen by fifty per cent. within the past seven years. In like manner the consumption of spirits in Sweden has declined over forty per cent. under the operation of the Bratt system.

The wets say that prohibition, designed to reduce alcohol consumption, has increased it; that it has bred a class of lawbreakers and converted a population of honest fishermen into sneaks and smugglers; and that the state's liquor excise revenues have been flung away for a system that enriches the bootlegger and encourages the contrabandier. The drys respond that patience is needed, that the right thing has been done, and that right will in the end prevail. The world must needs make haste slowly in the education of humanity to higher ideals of human conduct. Any great reform means the slow adaptation of the individual's inner life to the changed conditions of his external lot. In the meantime the prosperous Finnish bootlegger is entitled to say with boastful Glendower: "I can call up spirits from the vasty deep."

In conclusion one may ask why America did not produce a Bratt rather than a Volstead. In contrast to America, Sweden is a small country, with a homogeneous population. To what extent did conditions peculiarly Swedish determine the success of the Bratt experiment? Was Doctor Bratt more the creature than the creator of circumstance? As an American would he have proved a voice crying vainly in the wilderness, a prophet without disciples, a leader without followers? Could the Bratt system be worked in America? Who shall say?

# CHAPTER VIII

## FULLER CALLAWAY—COTTON PHILOSOPHER

FOLKS, meet Fuller E. Callaway, Georgia farmer, cotton spinner, village philosopher and whole-souled child of God. Knocking about Europe one meets cotton spinners in Milan, Italy; Lodz, Poland, or Manchester, England. It is not uncommon for the foreigner to inquire your place of residence in America. On one occasion the writer, feeling that his home town, Princess Anne, Maryland, might not be clearly visualized on the world map by a European, stated his place of residence as Baltimore. "Baltimore I know not," mused our foreign host, "but tell me how far is this place from Lah Grawnge, Georgia?" The local brakeman as the train approaches La Grange places the tonic accent upon the definite article and gives it the more flowery and poetic sound of Ley, as in the lay of the last minstrel—Ley Grainge, Ley Grainge. Alexandria, the home city of Cleopatra, Vaucluse, the retreat of Petrarch, La Grange, world famous as the home town of Fuller Callaway. Aside from being the home of Fuller Callaway, La Grange is an otherwise modest city of almost twenty thousand inhabitants by the census of 1930, distant by rail from Atlanta seventy-two miles and from Philadelphia eight hundred fifty miles.

My own introduction to Fuller Callaway came about in this fashion. As commercial attaché at the American Embassy, Rome, I was directed by cable from Washington to meet Callaway in Milan, introduce him to the local spinners, interpret his thoughts to the Italians and otherwise facilitate his mission. Mr. Callaway had come over to stir up enthusiasm among the Europeans for a great world cotton conference to be held in New Orleans. The British were hostile to the enterprise; the Continentals indifferent. Callaway went back home with European cooperation pledged up to the hilt and his cotton conference proved to be a huge success. No less than three hundred foreign delegates were sent to New Orleans. The morning after the conference adjourned seven Pullman trains pulled into La Grange, Georgia, discharging one thousand five hundred delegates. Callaway entertained the crowd at lunch at a village barbecue and later in the day Mrs. Callaway looked after about five hundred at a collation in her home. This is one reason why an inquisitive Pole or Italian will ask you vaguely how far Cleveland or St. Louis might be from La Grange, Georgia.

Some official jobs are less onerous and exacting than others. Although our friend Callaway landed in Milan entirely ignorant of the Italian language and without knowing a single human in the great city, the job of introducing him and acting as his interpreter was about as onerous as that of keeper of the canary bird-seed for the Grand Khan of Tartary. Before he had been in the city two hours our friend was surrounded by groups of fascinated Italians who swarmed about him as flies about a honey pot. Most of these men were in the cotton business and could speak English after a fashion, but whether they understood English or not seemed to make very little difference. Communication between human beings is not limited to spoken language. Dempsey did not have to know French to communicate with Carpentier or Spanish in order to reach an understanding with Firpo. There is a variety of means of expressing oneself. The star twinkles, the sun beams, a steam heater radiates. Callaway, twinkling, beaming, radiating among his fellows, needs no spoken language to make himself understood. The spoken word is not everything. Some human beings have the mysterious faculty of sensing what is going on in the minds of other people and impressing their ideas and personality upon their fellows. You can call it personality, human magnetism, but no matter where men like Callaway go they get what others have to give and they bestow what others desire to receive.

In his native town the language of Fuller Callaway is not the language of Edmund Burke or Walter Pater. Referring to the imperfections of his early academic training he remarks, "I had but two weeks' schooling in grammar. At the end of this period my teacher offered this counsel of desperation, 'Get your pappy to take you out in the smoke-house, make a good fire, strip off your clothes, pile the books around you, and you may possibly get some grammar in through your pores. You will never get any in through your head.'" So much for early education. We need not concern ourselves with that but rather with the method by which young Fuller laid hold of a wisdom which is beyond the knowledge obtained from all the schools. According to the chemical principle of endosmose and exosmose two liquids separated by a parchment pass through the partition and intermingle. So it is that homely wisdom has been a matter of give and take. Callaway has been a student all his life, and all his life in turn he has exuded that type of wisdom which is only another name for hard common sense.

Let us get away from the chattering, gesticulating, delighted group of Italians surrounding Callaway in Milan and in the words of the rustic presiding officer, "invoke a little quiescent quietude." Life in its humble, half-starved beginnings was quiet enough for young Fuller. He was one of fourteen children, the father a Baptist preacher in a sleepy southern town. Let us conservatively estimate the income and emoluments of a country parson in the impoverished South of the years succeeding the Civil War at five hundred dollars annually including pound parties, vegetable donations, bestowals of "freshies" at hog-killing time, not forgetting the Yuletide knitted socks and wristlets. Divide five hundred dollars by sixteen and the quotient expresses young Fuller's financial index and the urgent character of his impulse toward economic self-determination. At ten he was squarely out of the overcrowded family nest peddling spools of thread among the neighbors. At thirteen he had established himself as a cotton planter with a bit of rented land and a hired mule. He sold his first cotton crop at five and three-fourths cents per pound cleaning up thirty-six dollars and forty-five cents for the year's work. This money he put in the bank and has never finished taking it out. Later he came to own and operate one thousand five hundred acres of farm land. Side by side with farming he conducted on expanding scale some merchandising industry or other. He started in his native town a tiny five-and-ten-cent store which soon developed into a great enterprise. His whole life effort has been strung, so to say, on the thread of cotton fiber. To grow cotton, to twist the fiber into yarn and to sell cotton fiber either by hawking thread through the streets of his native village or later exporting it in the form of yarn or cotton piece goods to the far ends of the earth—this has been the vocation of Fuller Callaway.

I don't believe that any man who really knows him is a bit grudging or jealous of his success. Somebody desiring a short-cut to prosperity went to Callaway and asked him the secret of his success. Here is the reply poetically and succinctly set forth:

> "Late to bed,
> Early to rise.
> Work like hell
> And economize."

How much of Callaway's success is due to luck? Certainly his most brilliant achievement he modestly sets down to luck or what the old Calvinists used to call "abounding grace." At twenty he married Miss Ida Cason who had come to La Grange to pursue her education. In all the world nature could probably have designed no more exact complement and helpmeet for Callaway than what the accident of chance brought almost to his door. Mrs. Callaway, exhaling the perfume of human graciousness, runs their great house with its terraces, gardens and broad acres. If the lord of the manor unexpectedly brings home two guests they are welcome. If he should bring a hundred they too are welcomed and looked after, not only with the comforts which wealth provides but with unaffected kindness of heart.

Callaway will tell you of another piece of luck which came to him through meeting Kitchener in Egypt in February of 1913. Callaway did not need anybody to introduce him to Kitchener, he introduced himself and at once gave the great man advice as to how cotton should be raised in Egypt. The pink boll worm had become a great pest and the ignorant Egyptian peasants were unable to deal with it. "Why don't you grow an early maturing cotton that flowers before the pink worm can get in its work?" suggested Callaway.

"We grow a cotton now that matures in one hundred ten days," replied Kitchener.

"You can cut twenty-five per cent. off that time," observed Callaway.

"My plant biologists tell me the thing can not be done."

Callaway sitting in Kitchener's office wrote a cablegram to his manager at La Grange telling him to expedite five pounds of Truitt early maturing seed to Egypt. The following summer Kitchener cabled to Callaway at La Grange, Georgia: "Picking your cotton eighty-six days after seed were planted." In August, 1914, Callaway was in London when the Great War broke out and, unable to secure passage home, applied to his friend Kitchener. Kitchener booked him passage to New York and threw in this bit of advice: "Go back home, put up cotton mills and run them night and day. This war is going to last for years and the world will need all the cotton that you can possibly spin for it." Callaway went home and put up great mills which continued to work night and day for the better part of a decade. Incidentally he made a lot of money but money is not the thing which primarily interests Callaway. He often says, "I run my mills to pay the expenses of making American citizens."

The four or five thousand workers in his mills are Anglo-Saxons recruited from raw, ignorant

Americans back in the hills. Callaway employs neither negroes nor foreigners in his mills. He takes these crude young Americans from the hills, teaches them a useful handicraft and lifts them culturally the whole distance that lies between the seventeenth and the twentieth century. Callaway runs his mills on the patriarchal and paternal principle, under the principle whereby a father looking after his children expects the children in turn to look after him. A self-contained village life clusters about the Callaway mills. Community amusements, common pasturage for cows, Y. M. C. A.'s, schools presided over by principals that get better pay than a college professor in Yale or Princeton. This is what Callaway means by making money to make American citizens. The amount spent in community effort probably equals not less than four dollars and fifty cents as added to the weekly cash wage paid to labor. One result of all this is to educate labor out of the mills. The beams of light streaming in through the windows of a cotton mill reveal ten thousand motes and flecks of cotton suspended in the air. A dull tedious business tending looms and spindles and tolerable only to men of dull unimaginative minds. But, there are those who have with mental awakening the vision to see an angel standing in a beam of light. These boys press on for something better than jobs in the mills. So it is the stream keeps moving, the raw crude humanity recruited from the hills passing through Callaway's mills to a larger and ampler life. When the supply of native Anglo-Saxon labor has thus been exhausted, what next?

What is the key to the success of this man in dealing with his fellows, whether with a dull Georgia cracker or Lord Kitchener of Khartum? It's a quality, I think, of simple clear-eyed sincerity united with homely wisdom. The faith of the man has made him what he is—faith in God, country, humanity, faith too in himself. Callaway is descended from a long line of Baptist preachers, one of whom was born in Bedford County, Virginia, in 1712. Theologically Callaway is a throwback to the thirteenth century—to the days of Saint Bernard and Saint Francis of Assisi. His belief in the supernatural is as real as the presence of an automobile standing along the curb or a fire blazing in the grate. "I believe everything in the Bible—every word of it," he declares. "I never dispute with any one about religion. I am like my old Aunt Judy who was making pickles one day in the kitchen and had set a bowl of hot pickles outside to cool. One of our smart young men about

town dropped in to tell her that he had been reading some of the infidel writings and had decided to
give up his belief in the Bible. Aunt Judy did not
think it worth while to argue with him. All she
did was to throw the bowl of pickles in his face."
Our friend possesses probably the most distinct thir-
teenth-century theological mind in the state of
Georgia and he combines with it a moral quality
that makes him tell the whole truth as he sees it.
The last stronghold of conservatism in this country
is represented by men like Fuller Callaway. With
them it is the old-time theology, the old-time medicine and the old-time politics.

Callaway lives in a great mansion built in
Georgian style with "French" and "Italian" rooms
and period furniture, marble bird-baths on the
lawn and all the rest of it, but he is as simple and
ingenuous as a child about it all. Pointing to an
old Italian canvas on the wall which a professional
decorator had dug up from somewhere or other
he was wont to remark, "The thing looks like it
came out of a garbage can but I guess for anybody
who likes that kind of a thing that's about the
kind of a thing they would like." When the
great house was to be furnished the architect demanded to know where all the furniture was to
come from. "Plenty of it. Been collecting furni-

ture all my life. Hardly been a Saturday night in the last thirty years we haven't gone down to the village store and brought home furniture." The Callaway garden is one of the show places of the South: the old-type southern garden with its labyrinth of boxwood borders a hundred years old and with running vines climbing to the very top of magnolias and live oaks. Callaway loves birds, flowers, little children, and the scent of mother earth steaming up into his nostrils.

He can thrill you with interest while he sets you laughing.

"How short cotton fiber can you spin?"

"Anything that's got two ends to it," he answers. "What we can't spin we sell to stuff automobile cushions—stuff not good enough for stuffing we sell for wiping the automobile. The things we have no use for around our mills are waste, ignorance and grouch. The ignorant man is the only man I am afraid of. Educate a man and you can reason with him. We don't want men who are lean and sour. Contented women make contented households. We see to it that the homes of our workers have tight roofs and chimneys that draw. Housing has a great deal to do with human contentment. Some of our old southern homes had cavernous chimneys that took half the heat up the flue

Fuller Callaway

and sent half the smoke down into the dwelling.
A company dentist will pull an aching tooth for
twenty-five cents. A company mule driver will
plow the family garden for a nominal sum. If a
door sags or a window sticks the company's carpen-
ter drops in and fixes things. The surest way to
hold down labor turnover is to give the women
comfortable homes and little gardens. Our successful men cease to be successful when they begin
to want more than enough. A hog wanting more
than enough puts both his front feet in the trough
and keeps on eating. Not content, up comes the
left hind foot into the trough and over it goes. I
have had struggle and trouble enough to keep me
humble." He has worked from bitter poverty
and obscurity to amazing success and retains with
it all the humility and kindness of heart of earlier
days.

George Sand writing as a sentimentalist observed: "In this ill-regulated world of ours, all
happiness seems a theft since we can not enjoy
our peace and security except to the detriment of
our fellow creatures." There is a fallacy in the
sentiment and Callaway is ready to prove it. It
is tolerably certain that man may not only rise to
place and fortune in our western democracy without doing hurt to his fellow mortals, but he may

actually build into the structure of his own success the happiness and well being of myriads of his fellow creatures. Benjamin Franklin in his day best expressed the genius and character of the American people. His life with its early merciless buffetings and half-starved beginnings blossomed into world-wide influence and success. But suffering such as would have sufficed to narrow and sour many a man left him one of the kindest, most generous and most unassuming of mortals. Theologically Callaway is thirteenth century, philosophically he is of the pioneering, self-reliant, homespun era of our national infancy. Industrially he is in the van of our energetic, aspiring complex twentieth-century life. He symbolizes the new South roused from its inertia, its preoccupation with politics, plunging eagerly and manfully into the swift current of modern competitive business. Callaway's doings are an enigma to quacks, cowards and insincere persons.

# CHAPTER IX

## Getting Booth Tarkington Educated

An interval of thirty-six years—a mere trifle in the existence of the fixed stars, counts heavily in the life of the human biped. Looking back across this chasm of time, I recall Booth Tarkington on a Princeton Commencement Day lounging dejectedly in his college room while his more forward-looking classmates were receiving their diplomas from the trembling hands of the venerable Chairman of the Board of Trustees. I sat by Tark—everybody called him Tark—through this painful crisis as one would sit by the bedside of a fever-stricken patient. The only time in his college course that Tark set any store upon a diploma was the morning of Commencement Day when the sheepskins were awarded. Though Tarkington never applied himself slavishly to study in college he managed to absorb enough classroom lore to slide through examinations with credit. He had prepared for a scientific course in college but switched on entering Princeton to the so-called classical or bachelor of arts course. He lacked Greek and it was this lack that afflicted him on

Commencement Day, but on no other day before or since. President Patton in Tark's time was already challenging Greek as an indispensable requirement for a Princeton A.B. Tark, it seemed, was a little ahead of his time. Greek presently ceased to be required by Princeton for an A.B. degree.

Not so many months ago, fresh from vacationing at White Sulphur Springs where he had steadily worked some twelve hours a day on his latest novel, Tark met me in Washington. He was clearly flustered and outdone. "I can't go to my summer place in Kennebunkport on account of college commencements. They book me for honorary degrees every year. I hate to go up on the platform. I am sick of this degree business," he muttered, his hand trembling with more than its habitual palsy as he lighted another cigarette.

Tarkington has been bemastered and bedoctored until he looks on a college commencement platform as a malefactor regards the gallows on which he is to be hanged. But there he is, whimpering, shivering like a wet hound on an ice floe, doomed to occupy a platform for the rest of his life.

So it was that the non-hellenic Tarkington, the most brilliant man of his generation in Princeton, did not ascend the commencement platform when his class graduated in 1893. Nobody was much concerned about it as we had him marked for an early grave. He fooled us most delightfully. Yet we had reason on our side. Tark, with his sallow skin, stooped shoulders and hollow cough, displayed all the stigmata of extreme nicotine poisoning. The taint of sin as well as the perils of poison attached to cigarette-smoking thirty-five years ago. Ministers of the Gospel preached against cigarettes and "the dance" as works of the Devil. Cigarettes were said to contain "dope." That cigarettes were clearly destroying Tark's nerves, paralyzing his will and enfeebling his intellect was as clear as a proposition in Euclid. I once figured out to my own satisfaction that the stones of the great pyramid at Ghiseh would load to maximum capacity a solid train of forty-foot steel gondola cars reaching from New York to Chicago. Now let some mathematician compute the linear distance, if they were laid end to end, of the cigarettes smoked by Tark in forty years. We gave Tark short of a year to live unless he quit cigarettes. But after forty years he hasn't cut down either cigarettes or work, and to-day possesses a greater capacity for sustained literary effort than any man I have ever known. If put to it, he can out-talk, out-write, out-drink any of his contemporaries. Aforetime he didn't employ a secretary to assist him in his liter-

ary output but wrote down every word himself
and could keep at it for fourteen hours on a stretch
if some one were good enough to bring him a little
food and water in between times. If this isn't hard
work, what is? Even the mechanical part of writing is hard work; to this the pain of thinking must
be added, for to write without thinking is vain in
these latter days.

Tark appeared in Princeton as a junior, entering
the class of '93. He was sponsored by Big Murray,
a blond giant designed as a darling of nature to be
the model for a collar ad or matinée idol in a
moving-picture show. His fame too would not
have suffered in the talkies. I had graduated the
preceding June and was back on a history fellowship, mistakenly bent on carving out a career as
a scholar. My room was about fifty paces distant
from apartment numbered "U" in University Hall
occupied by Murray and Tarkington. I had spent
four years climbing the academic ladder; had enjoyed such rank as editor-in-chief of the college
paper, membership on prize-debating teams, and
now was back in Princeton shorn of every vestige
of dignity and authority. "Gigmanity disgigged,"
as Carlyle describes the gig-driving French aristocrats who lost everything in the Revolution. My
friend Murray introduced me to his new roommate

soon after he got to Princeton. When presented, Tark was squatted on one end of a sofa munching doughnuts, drinking beer, fiddling with pencil and paper. "He's sketching," cried Big as if he were showing off a trained animal. There was something gnome-like about this odd figure of a man. The lustrous eyes and Savonarola mouth suggested the venerable domesticated carp which obtrude their nozzles in the pools of Fontainebleau. His grin disclosed the stained and darkened teeth of an octogenarian. He gestured by pawing with incredulous suspicion at his indeterminate chin. His fine lustrous eyes fully redeemed other facial debits. Eyes that were pools of intelligence. But we little suspected how deep these pools were or what lay concealed in their shadowy depths. Yes, there was something rather pathetic about Tark at first look—this cadaverous, sunken-chested fellow with his hunched-over shoulders, turned out in poisonously ugly yellowish brown Harris tweeds and shoes with fancy cloth uppers. But he had something better than pretty looks—he had savor, instant magnetism.

We knew him first as a delightful waster and slacker. As Macaulay wrote of Horace Walpole, serious business was a trifle to him and trifles were his serious business. To compose little verses on

[ 277 ]

trivial subjects, to decorate sheets of paper with absurd drawings, to tinkle a guitar, to bicker importantly about unimportant matters, to rehearse for a college comedy, to indite an appropriate mot on a lady's fan—these were his serious academic employments. As was said of a delightful trifler "he had every talent except the talent of making use of his talents." Tark seldom rose before ten, breakfasting in his room on left-overs from the preceding night's frolic. Some fidus Achates could usually be depended upon to fill his seat at morning prayers. His elective studies were chosen on the principle of bunch and cinch; courses bunched for convenience in evading them, a cinch for convenience in passing examinations. Certain professors were known to have bowels of compassion, sharing the amiable philosophy of Charles II that God will not damn a mortal for taking a little pleasure out of the way.

If Tark ever did any classroom work it was done furtively and without boasting. His electives bore no relation to any common objective. They were as incoherent as primordial chaos. From his reference to the art of the early Etruscans it would appear that he was a patron of a course in the history of the fine arts. Other references indicated that he was pursuing a course in the Harmony of Science and Religion offered by a retired Presbyterian clergyman. The name of this revered professor was held in blessed esteem because of the flowery reputation of never having flunked any student in any examination. Two schools of thought had developed as to the validity of his teachings. Some held that "the old gentleman had made good in establishing Harmony." Others thought that "he had fallen down on Harmony." Tark, with his mental integrity to maintain, very properly refused to take sides. "I can't commit myself," he maintained, "without hearing some of the evidence."

Tark never mentioned his curriculum undertakings, but he did absorb something if only through the pores of the skin while waiting in tortured suspense for the bell that would release him from the classroom. His books are rich in allusions to the classic world; he analyzes social problems as if he had made a systematic study of them. The fact remains that he is a man of broad culture; how he acquired it is another matter. His mind was not made to be clogged with the relevancies or irrelevancies of the odd bits of information dinged into us at college, such as the Binomial theorem—blue litmus paper turning red—use of the second for the first aorist—Theodoric the Ostrogoth—rule in Shelley's case—the forged decretals—struggle over the investiture—peace of Westphalia—prepositions governing the accusative—the categorical imperative. Facts may be stored up in the attic of one's mind like the odd sizes of lumber in a mill yard. A customer comes for a bill of material and you have all sizes except the ones stipulated in the bill. Tark never read anything in college—that is we never caught him reading anything—and yet he justly passed for a well-read man. He has no children. Where did he learn the intimate secrets of children's lives? He has always been essentially a man's man. How does he come to know the innermost depths of women's souls?

Back in the Dark Ages, men found miracles a convenient explanation for phenomena they did not understand. Gifted men of the antique world were also accredited with the gift of divination or the gift of tongues. Let this fiction serve for Tark as for other gifted mortals whom we can't explain in terms of our own more limited intelligence. We of lesser breed have to struggle for the light; have to be told how; have to be educated by lectures rammed down our throats. Tark neglected college professors who lectured on literature. It was his destiny to make English literature rather than learn about it. Does a man become more eupeptic from knowing all about the processes of digestion? More, a man may be a good wood-chopper without being able to describe the process, and a college professor may talk wisely about the art of chopping wood without being able to chop wood himself. Tark obtained from Princeton things that are better than utility and more valuable than book learning. In the confraternity of Princeton men, he came to know his fellow mortals; he learned tolerance; he came to see that no man was too poor or too obscure to be exempt from his consideration. He learned that being a man nothing human was foreign to him.

It is the fashion to look back on the Princeton of thirty-five years ago as a delightful country club where we had our sports, our comradeships, our teeming little delightful activities. President Patton, replying to the charge that Princeton had become a blessed resort for loafers, paraphrased Tennyson in the couplet:

"It is better to have come and loafed
Than never to have come at all."

This was the lawyer's plea of confession and avoidance. Later when a plan was bruited for

[ 281 ]

stiffening up the curriculum, an aggrieved alumnus is reported to have complained, "They are trying to make a damned educational institution out of the place." It all depends on what a man means by education and what he proposes to do with it. If he desires to be instructed in the utilitarian arts of pickle packing, tripe tasting, ice-cream freezing, Princeton is not and never was an educational institution. Don't ask poets to write bills of lading, or painters to whitewash fences, or paleontologists to gather bones for glue factories. De Musset was not made for the delicatessen shop nor Shelley for selling patent churns.

As humanity comes up from savagery and emerges from the mere animal struggle for existence, two faculties develop: first, intellectual curiosity, which is the beginning of all learning; second, the esthetic instinct or the love of beauty, which is the beginning of all art. The Princeton of our day was the seed-bed for the quickening of these two faculties. Princeton takes a raw crude lad and without necessarily making him either a great scientist, classical scholar, philosopher, historian or political economist, by some alchemy transforms him into a man of culture. We don't know exactly how this is accomplished, anymore than we know how a catalyst works in

a chemical reaction. We know that pure hydro-
gen may be made to combine with atmospheric
nitrogen through the use of a catalyst and that
out of the union a precious plant food, ammonia,
may be produced synthetically.

I think of Princeton under the image of a catalyst. Princeton takes the raw coarse elements in
a man and combines them into a finer product.
The awakening to beauty is a good part of it
whether we concede it or not. The external beauty
of the place—seniors singing in the soft May twi-
light on the steps of Old North—the beauty of
intellect—the minds of such men as Doctor Patton and Professor Woodrow Wilson, capable of
spinning the gossamers as well as forging the steel
girders of thought—the beauty of holiness, if you
will, as we sat together years ago in Marquand
Chapel—the beauty of a goal kicked from the
thirty-five-yard line—"Old Nassau" chanted by
massed multitudes—the beauty of comradeship—
the beauty of culture itself—the discovery of
things that are more precious than profit, that are
more valuable than market price.

One naturally thinks in terms of his own experience. I recall coming up to Princeton from
the isolated life of a southern plantation. It was
like stepping into an ampler world. And it meant

an ampler world too for city-bred Booth Tarkington. The world moves and Princeton with it. No doubt a man acquires better book learning in the new Princeton, but I doubt if he acquires finer inspirations than did the old-timers when the college was one-fourth the size in numbers. Our teeming human ant-hill bred heroes a-plenty. The hero who was let down by a rope from the top of the water-tower to paint class numerals on its sheer expanse—the hero who had stolen the clapper from the bell in Old North that summoned us to morning prayers and recitations—the heroes of cane rushes, snowball fights. Heroic defenders of the good old customs. Some of these good old customs, by the way, dated back as much as five years. These hero days were also the days of the college hoax. Tommie Bell had us all agog over his famous counterfeiting hoax. For days on end, we sensed the veiled presence of Secret Service men about to rip the lid from a pious educational institution to reveal an undercover gang engaged in counterfeiting the good and lawful money of the United States. This same Tommie Bell wrought the whole college to a fever of apprehension over the pseudo dead body of a murdered person reported in Tommie's bedroom. Perhaps Bell's cadaver hoax suggested Tark's spooky spiritualistic seances in Room U. Tradition had it that a beautiful maiden crossed in love had committed suicide in Room U when University Hall was a hotel. A dark stain on the floor of Tark's apartment was pointed out as authentication of the tragedy, just as the stain of Lord Darnley's blood may be descried on the floor of Holyrood Castle. Tark rigged a mechanical contrivance which by slowly raising his arm would lower the gas-jets until only a blue ring remained. A clicking electrical contrivance was installed in his bedroom. Getting hold of a "subject" who professed not to believe in spiritualism, Tark undertook to materialize the suicide's departed spirit. In the dim uncertain light with answers clicked out on his apparatus, the apparition in the form of a confederate appeared from a folding couch. The act went over big.

Of course, such goin's-on would be considered bad form nowadays. Collegiatism has lost its creativeness. Chiefly, I think, because it has lost its capacity to be thrilled. Automobiles, movies, other reliefs to the tedium of study hours have come in. Sartorially, we were content in three-dollar corduroy trousers. The present generation goes hand-tailored; mind-tailored too for that matter. The prevailing model calls for quiet styles—something above all that will not betray the individual as a college man. The prevailing tone just now is one of decorous dullness. It is bad form to get maniacal over a goal from the field from the thirty-five-yard line. Dignified Chesterfieldian detachment—decorous dullness. So looking back through the golden haze of years, one laments the degeneracy of the times just as the rich Biblical landowner lamented two thousand years ago that "things are not what they once were."

Jesse Lynch Williams claimed to have brought Tark out as a writer. I suppose some venerable village blacksmith also claims to have "learned Henry Ford when a boy all about mechanical contraptions."

Somebody it seemed wrote to Jesse to look up Tarkington when the latter arrived in Princeton and "be nice" to the newcomer. Jesse was of the patrician breed, a member of the senior class and a man with an established literary reputation. It took some grace and condescension on his part to glad-hand this queer western person with the curious name; but Jesse was always man-square in every emergency. Faithful to his obligation, he took Tark up and later got him to write some stuff for the *Nassau Lit,* all of which was on a par with teaching a duck how to swim. Only a few years before, when Jesse entered college as a freshman, I had the same experience greeting him that he had with welcoming Tarkington. Our mothers being dear friends and former schoolmates, I was charged to be "kind and good to Bettie Riddle's boy." As a sophomore, I dutifully took up freshman Jesse, found him a quiet, brown-faced, peaceable-minded lad and about as easy to patronize as the Archbishop of Canterbury. If Tark gave the impression of loafing, Jesse conveyed the impression of sauntering through life. I fell in with Jesse one morning sauntering along McCosh Walk, stooping once in a while to pluck wild violets. "I am gathering these for a far-away friend," he remarked dreamily.

"If you mean some girl," I broke in, "why not send her something worth-while. These wild violets are as common as sin and they have no perfume."

"They will have an uncommonness and a perfume too," he remarked, "for the recipient when she knows where and by whom they were gathered."

That was Jesse self-revealed; a man who could take the commonplace things of life and endow them with rarity and perfume.

It just happened that Tark needed no introductions. He picked up friends as a woolly sheep collects cockleburs. A stocky, red-faced, sporting character named George Benham, Burnham or something (the last name is of no more social significance than the family name of King Amnnullah of Afghanistan) kept a pool-room on Nassau Street fairly opposite the college campus. An enchanting taint of sin hung about this sporting resort; betting was said to go on there. George himself was accredited with a sixth sense in divining the issues of all sporting events. The ancient Romans divined the future by resorting to the haruspices who read the future by inspecting the entrails of newly killed animals. For our divinations, we went direct to George or else to Helldiver Skillman, a similarly gifted Townie. Many are alive to-day who will tell you that Helldiver never once incorrectly forecast the issue of a Princeton-Yale football game. Until a man had risen out of the common ruck of humanity along toward his senior year, he could hope for no social recognition from George, the gifted billiard marker. George was not of the blood royal, but was king by right of the ascendency which strong natures exercise over the weak. To have George call you by your name and to be able to address him on terms of equality as "George," was the social equivalent of a card from the British Lord Chamberlain admit-

*Of a Sunday Night in February*
*1894*

My dear Lennis,—

This is Sunday and ⟶ This ⟵ is Me. I have just returned from Church. I go every Sunday with Ma. I am getting to be too exemplary for any use. I like to talk about myself first.

What in the world struck you and Povie? I know if I had been there to superintend your diet you'd have quite well all year. I have changed my old night lunch a bit. If you will follow my plan you'll never have another bad day. Between two and five A.M. every night take unlimited Beer Bananas, Cheese Sandwiches, Chocolate creams and Cake, Lemon Tee and a Welsh Rarebit. Don't go to bed too early. This is the secret of my constitution.

Truly, here in the ever lands spring

Letter from Tarkington to the author, written from Indianapolis in February, 1894, the year after he left Princeton. A delightful, unstudied letter with not a serious word in it

has same, the leaves are wooed by the mellow sun
even as Forsyth was wooed and won by the Maid
of Chicago that I vainly loved last year — the foliage
like a bud at her first tea is in its earliest
blush. When the blossoms are glorious, when the
moon makes of summer evenings a wandering
nocturne and the air breathes a low symphonic
music and the birds croon love-songs in thick
foliage, O Dennis, when all maids are fair
and all men young — when life is a sweet
sweet dream and all things drool in honeyed
low-voicedness and the breeze is scented
— in short O Dennis, in June — come to
Good Old Indianapolis and Visit Me.
           y
       Yours For Keeps.
           Newton Booth Tarkington

( I've got a new silk 'at —
a ate dollar one — next
one I'll spend thirteen )

Cut this
out and
present it to the
senior class from a bull-wrinkler as a
testimonial of his
affection. Cupid.

ting the bearer to the Royal Enclosure at Ascot.

When Tark was barely a month in college, I fell in step with him one day as we were passing the pool-room. George's face lighted with kindly benevolence. "Howdy-do, Tark!" he saluted. "Howdy-do, George!" grinned Tark, as little flustered as if he were speaking to one of the college tutors! TARK WAS CALLING BENHAM "GEORGE" WITHIN A MONTH AFTER ENTERING COLLEGE! The man was simply amazing. Herbert Spencer defines happiness as the establishment of harmony between one's inner aspirations and one's external lot. Tark was perfectly at home and perfectly happy in any society in any environment. He is the only man of my time who was editor of both the *Lit* and the *Tiger* simultaneously. He wrote stories for the *Lit* and did cartoons for the *Tiger*. He was also a member of both the Glee and Dramatic Clubs at the same time. In collaboration with Post Wheeler, Tark wrote a travesty on Julius Cæsar for the Dramatic Club, assisted in mounting the play and enacted the part of Brutus when the play was presented. On the Glee Club, he became chief soloist. Eugene Cowles' magnificent bass in the Jet Black Crow song was a feature of *Robin Hood*, the popular light opera of the day. When it was found that Tark could go farther down cellar than Cowles in singing the doleful ditty, he became what the French call a *succès fou* as a campus singer. His singing of Kipling's *Danny Deaver* was unique as a dramatic tour de force. At senior singing, everybody cried out for *Danny Deaver,* and poor Tark would be drawn forth whimpering and protesting much like the passing soul of the unfortunate Danny and made to do his mournful stuff.

Goaded on by Jesse Williams, Tark turned in filler for the *Lit* as a hack writer turns out copy to pay a coal bill. But the stuff made no great impression. The delightful humor of *Seventeen,* the dramatic evocations of the past as in *Beaucaire* were not there. One trouble, I think, was his excessive popularity. The best writing is done in quiet places. Tark, like a pilot fish drawing his school of little fishes with him, converted scholarly retreats into the clamant places of the world. One may talk before a crowd, sing before a crowd, but not write for publication before a crowd. Tark had about as much privacy in his apartment as Louis XIV at his morning rising when twoscore persons stood about the royal bedside for the ceremony of enrobing the royal personage with the royal shirt. The little group of familiars were a constant social quantity to which was added the

variable "X" consisting of casual callers to whom
looking up with an inquiring glance Tark might
have conceivably inquired, "To what am I indebted
for the honor of your visit at this ungodly hour
of the night?" It was hard for the popular Murray
to be eclipsed by his protégé, Tark, just as it was
hard for the artist Cimabue to be outdone by his
pupil Giotto. Still Cimabue was almighty proud
of Giotto. Murray was a living illustration of the
injustice that withholds from the man who pays
the piper the privilege of calling the tune.

Murray has been heard to express a desire to
bone up for an exam; but the evening sessions in
Room U rarely broke up before one or two o'clock
in the morning and frequently the light in Tark's
room would be glowing at sunrise. There was
no order about this apartment except its disorder.
Empty cigarette boxes strung on threads attached
to the picture molding criss-crossed beneath the
ceiling and looped in festoons about the chandelier.
What was the ontology of these countless empty
cigarette boxes? Did they satisfy the collector's
passion for the rare and unattainable; were they
displayed as trophies; as warnings; or as decora-
tions? It was the age for collecting bric-à-brac.
It was considered chic supreme to cover the walls
with incongruous signs swiped from barrooms, rail-

the little chains he wears around his neck." Howard
Butler, another one of the group, became a famous
archeologist. Jesse Carter, perhaps after Tark the
most distinguished member of the class of 1893,
seldom appeared at meetings in Room U, having
a reputation for profound scholarship to sustain.
Carter became known to classical scholars throughout the world. He lies beneath the cypresses in
the Protestant cemetery at Rome hard by the graves
of Shelley and Keats. McCready Sykes earned
distinction with his pen and Jesse Lynch Williams
for a generation has been known to America as
a man of letters. Covington, Bradshaw, Carter,
Butler, George Benham, Jesse Lynch Williams are
dead; and Tark, destined as one believed to die
young, goes on with undiminished zest for life and
unabated capacity to meet its demands.

Tark never was known to hurry out of his
shambling shuffling walk, never perspired, smoked
incessantly, ate immoderately, violated every canon
of health. His favorite midnight lunches were of
caviar, candy, doughnuts, hard cider, welsh rarebit, cream puffs, bananas. No one ever heard Tark
complain of headache, indigestion, fatigue or the
inclemency of the weather. His great success in
life was built as much around his stomach as around
his head. Anemic, sniggering, shuffling Tark out-

stays us all in either work or play. While he can drink almost any man under the table, it has now come about that he drinks alcohol not at all. Twenty years ago some one asked Tark when he was going to quit drinking. "I'm not going to quit," he replied, "I have quit!"

When the iridescent winged butterflies came fluttering to Princeton for the proms and football games, Murray was in his element. The handsome of the earth are the darlings of college proms. Such affairs are peopled by Ephemeridæ evaluated for that one evening by externals. Beauty seeks beauty. Let some queer-looking fellow aspire to have his name inscribed on the dance card of one of these reigning beauties—he'd be lucky to get the third extra of the twentieth number with a chance in the interim to lumber around the ballroom two or three times with some heavy chaperon. There were chaperons in those days just as there were beautiful pale faces. At a dance nobody cared about Tark's skill at bickering or his rendition of *Danny Deaver*, and his position as a pleasure-seeker may be depicted in the words of Walter Bagehot, "Misery trying to be gay; gaiety feeling itself to be miserable." The woes of the timid stripling at a dance are set forth in more than one of Tark's stories.

And so Tark, celebrated fribbler, went out into the world and was apparently swallowed up into oblivion. About a year after his departure from Princeton, my classmate, Roy Goldsbury, stopping over in Indianapolis, made inquiry of a prominent citizen as to the particular niche Tark was occupying in his home town. The subject of the inquiry replied wearily, "Oh, we all know him and love him but he will never amount to anything, piddling around and smoking himself to death." And then came in quick succession his *Gentleman from Indiana, Beaucaire, The Two Vanrevels*, and with these instant fame for the local piddler. This, by the way, marked the period when our finest scholar, a man who had led our class for the entire four years in Princeton, published his Doctor's Thesis entitled *The Gruhasangraha—Parisishta of Gobila-putra.*

And Tarkington, after thirty years his natural force unabated, picturizes with facile brain men and women we lesser mortals see every day of our lives without understanding them. Except for a dimming of those wise, all-seeing eyes, his capacity for work is undiminished, the creative zest unabated. Beneath a passive exterior his mind moves with the incessant activity of an imprisoned insect—yes, with the invincible obstinacy of an insect.

Years ago we were marching shoulder to shoulder up and down Nassau Street cheering, singing, rejoicing noisily in our strong young lives. Over in the museum of Old North stood skeletons of mighty extinct animals. These animals also had their little day as they gamboled and cavorted in the primeval ooze, rejoicing noisily in their fruitless lives.

Thirty-five years ago life seemed to hold so much for us—the unbounded expectations, the intimations of greatness, and now the meager results, the hopes turned to memories. Some of the men who took high places in their college studies have made no great figure in the world. Tarkington, who made an indifferent showing as a student, has created a great name for himself in the world. A name like to outlive that of any Princeton man of his day. Now, having achieved fame and fortune, why doesn't he take a little rest? What goads him on? There is no answer unless it be the creative instinct of the artist. The instinctive urge to produce something that will live afterward. Won't Tarkington, reviewing the much spent inheritance of life, tell us what it is all about? "I haven't time," he would say, "for such abstractions. I want a new speed boat and must write a story forthwith to pay for it." That is the whimsical Tark. He doesn't mean it—he'd tell us the answer if he could.

[ 297 ]

# CHAPTER X

## PUDDLER JIM

IT SEEMS almost a sacrilege to speak of the Honorable James John Davis, Secretary of Labor in three Cabinets, Director General of the Loyal Order of Moose, senator elect from the grand old state of Pennsylvania, as "Puddler Jim," but Mr. Davis himself will have it that way. Iron puddling is the central theme in his delightful autobiography and he likes to have his friends call him Jim. There is nothing offish or high-hattish about plain Jim Davis, and that's one reason why the one-time poor little Welsh immigrant boy became head of our National Immigration Service, why he has been translated from a mill-town shanty in western Pennsylvania to a beautiful home in Washington, and why, after a long apprenticeship in the murky, super-heated atmosphere of a puddling furnace, he is headed for the delightfully cooled, warmed, ventilated and rarefied atmosphere of the United States Senate chamber.

The success curve of Mr. Davis displays an unbroken upward trajectory covering a period of some forty or more years. Shallow thinkers speak of him as a lucky man, but is success over a period of forty years, whether in cards, love, the stock market, business or the learned professions, a matter of luck? The behaviorists will tell you that a man succeeds because it's implicit in his nature. He simply follows the larval instinct to struggle upward to the light. The lowly grub crawls out of the earth and becomes an iridescent-winged creature of the air. Thus it is that a man builds his success just as a robin instinctively fashions its nest.

The writer having known Mr. Davis at close range, it may be worth while to consider in a scholarly, workmanlike fashion how he has come to be what he is. Deep thinkers have their own methods of getting at the truth. Some set great store by the historical method. They seek an answer to every riddle in a study of past experience. Others put the emphasis on perspective, thus relying on the comparative method. If you want to estimate an individual, line him up in relation to his fellows. Others go in for the psychological method, estimating what a man is by what he thinks. The writer, in his poor, amateurish, humble way, without making any pretense to a profound knowledge of metaphysics, the Mendelian Law, the rule in Shelley's case, or the Kantian doctrine of the categorical imperative, will try to present the Honorable James J. Davis as he was and as he is.

Let us first, then, after the manner of deep thinkers, apply the historical method:

Chronological Table:

Born October 27, 1873, in a two-room brick-row cottage in Tredegar, Wales.

Poverty-stricken immigrant to America and shanty dweller in Pennsylvania mill town at the age of eight.

Bootblack and messenger boy at nine.

Assistant iron puddler in Pennsylvania mill town at eleven.

Clarinet tooter in mill-town band at thirteen.

Full-blown iron puddler at sixteen.

Home-run batter on local nine at seventeen.

Cook and roustabout in southern peonage camp at eighteen.

Tin roller in mills of Tin Plate King Reid at twenty.

Head of local labor union at twenty-two.

City clerk in Elwood, Indiana, at twenty-five.

County Recorder at twenty-nine.

Director General Loyal Order of Moose at thirty-three.

Capitalist at thirty-five.

Secretary of Labor, Harding Cabinet, at forty-seven.

Secretary of Labor, Coolidge Cabinet, at forty-nine.

Secretary of Labor, Hoover Cabinet, at fifty-five.

United States Senator-Elect from Pennsylvania at fifty-six.

This is simply the bare scaffolding; we'll have to fill in a bit or two. When young Jim Davis was dragged feet first, kicking and protesting, from his ancestral home in Wales to embark for America as a steerage passenger, along with his mother and her five small children, he laid hold of the plank floor and bore away in his tight little fist splinters from the ancestral home. They were following a father who had gone to America some months ahead to improve the family fortunes. The old gentleman never learned to read and write, but it would be a mistake to set him down as an illiterate. He had a native store of common sense and intelligence that is more essential to good citizenship than the learning of the schools. Shortly after landing in America he made an emphatic cross mark by way of signing his application for naturalization. Mrs. Davis succeeded in piloting her six children, all under twelve years, to Sharon, a Pennsylvania mill town. The feather-bed, the dean of the family furnishings, was stolen during the voyage.

[ 301 ]

Two of the six children strayed away in the streets of New York and were lost for days. The family resources were entirely exhausted in an effort to recover the children. Some benevolent gentleman took up a collection and saw them through their difficulties. Barring these misadventures, the passage to America was uneventful.

The Davises in Sharon, Pennsylvania, like the Coolidges in Northampton, Massachusetts, occupied the hither end of a double frame house, with this difference—the Sharon home was an unpainted shanty which possessed about all the modern conveniences and luxuries of an Aleutian Island wickiup.

Some men are born to riches, education, social position. These pampered mortals are not goaded by the primal instinct to struggle upward. They are up before they start. "God gave them their request, but sent leanness into their soul," writes the Psalmist. Young Jim had little to start with, but he had richness of soul. He was of genuine stuff, strong, lusty, plebeian, full of pluck, full of patience, full of good nature. While yet a stripling he crept forth in the gray hours of the morning from a Pennsylvania mill-town shanty to give the strength of his youth to hard muscular labor. Fate, it seemed, had condemned him to penal servitude at hard labor in a beautiful world of freedom where children frolic and play, get their proper schooling, and live with no more care or responsibility for their keep than the lilies of the field. Early sufferings and privations such as would have warped and soured a nature second to his, only served to make him one of the kindest, most amiable, most sympathetic of mortals.

Years of labor as an iron puddler in the searing heat of the molten metal left no more mark upon him than did King Nebuchadnezzar's burning, fiery furnace upon Shadrach, Meshach and Abednego. Time, with its labors, its anxieties, its struggles, etches as with a corroding acid the lineaments of men who struggle upward out of poverty and obscurity to the heights. The do-nothings are also marked by time; they degenerate like the penguins, which, having lost their power of flight, waddle and flounder. Few men come into the world with so rich a heritage of mental and physical health as Jim Davis. His superb physique found its complement in perfect adaptation to the muscular job of iron puddler. Jim Davis was born with the potential strength of a prize fighter, and, like a prize fighter, he can take a stiff blow on the chin and come up smiling. He has come up fast, just as a man with sturdy legs can beat an escalator by leaping up three steps at a time while the contraption is slowly ascending. Young Jim Davis asked not so much for happiness as for an opportunity to exercise his capacities. No job was too humble or exacting. He did about everything a boy can do in a mill town to turn an honest penny. He blacked other people's shoes, ran other people's errands, carried other people's parcels.

Young Davis was a child without any self-pity, with an inextinguishable gusto for life and its activities. He got an education, but he didn't get it from the schools. "Labor," he wrote in afterlife, "is the foundation of all true knowledge; handicraft is the basis of the best schooling." He got an abundant education out of the handicrafts, learning two trades—iron puddling and tin rolling—before he was twenty-one. How much intelligence goes into these jobs one is not prepared to estimate, but iron puddling means stirring a charge of viscous molten iron with a twenty-five-pound iron rake for ten hours in a room as hot as the stokehole of an ocean liner. A man may have the will for such work, but not one in a hundred has the physical stamina. Jim Davis had both—liked his job, gloried in it, applied to it all the fierce energy of his powerful young body.

During the hard times of the early 'nineties, mills

shut down, jobs were scarce and money hard to come by. Young Davis became a tramp looking for a job instead of the conventional tramp trying to avoid a job. Laid off at home, he went to Pittsburgh, thence to Birmingham, Alabama. His fellow lodgers in a Birmingham boarding-house house known as The Bucket of Blood objected to his burning the lamp for midnight reading and expressed their disapproval by throwing him bodily out of a second-story window. From Birmingham he drifted to Louisiana, and was greeted on arrival by a lanky southerner. "You-all are coming down hyah lookin' for food and work. In 'sixty-five you was down hyah lookin' for blood." Jim found blood in a peonage camp where he was put to work driving a mule hitched to a dirt scraper. Becoming entangled with the mule and the dirt scraper, Jim emerged bruised and bleeding, and was discharged on the spot as an incompetent, with no pay other than an application of horse liniment to his wounds. From Louisiana he tramped and bummed rides on freight trains to Elwood, Indiana, where he got a job in Daniel Reid's tin-plate mills. In course of time he came to be chief of the local union, kept the men out of foolish strikes, won a place in the hearts of bosses and fellow laborers. A solid package of self-expression, he sang his way, talked his way, clarineted his way into popularity. But Fate handed him some stiff rebuffs. Handy with his fists, he found plenty of use for them. One day he knocked out the village bully for ridiculing his hand-me-down pants. Another time he settled accounts by wiping up the floor of a newspaper office with the local editor. When he got to be city clerk of Elwood, he established contact with a crooked paving contractor by giving the man a beating which sent him to the hospital. In Mr. Davis' own words: "I grew into manhood with muscled arms as big as a bookkeeper's legs." If any one desires to settle a dispute with Mr. Davis, he would do well not to appeal to the arbitrament of fists.

Mr. Davis' campaign speeches for city clerk lacked the verbal nicety and elegance which distinguish the diction of Walter Pater and Edmund Burke, but he employed language that even the village idiot could understand. There was only one confusion of language in the campaign. He put out cards inscribed, "Jas. J. Davis." This confused many voters who knew him only as "Jim."

In course of time the poverty-stricken little immigrant boy becomes chief of the National Immigration Service. Mr. Davis came to enjoy the distinction of holding a Cabinet position under three Presidents. The late James Wilson, of Iowa, and Mr. Davis' fellow townsman, Andrew W. Mellon, of Pittsburgh, are the only other Americans in our history that have served in the Cabinets of three administrations.

The Comparative Method:

The merits of this method are obvious. A man's position in the world of space and time is established by his relation to other objects in the universe. The sailor establishes his position at sea by his relation to the sun and the stars. Following this method, a comparison may be set up between Mr. Davis and Mr. Coolidge. Both exemplify uninterrupted success in American politics. Mr. Coolidge was born on July fourth, which augured well for a public career, just as Mr. Davis, almost contemporaneously, was born on October twenty-seventh, Theodore Roosevelt's birthday. Mr. Coolidge, arriving on this planet a little ahead of Mr. Davis, kept ahead of him, and of course will remain ahead of him, since Mr. Davis, by reason of his foreign nativity, is constitutionally barred from the White House. As to early advantages, Mr. Coolidge had much that Mr. Davis hadn't, including a fair competence, a college education, leisure to read and to cultivate his mind. On the physical side Mr.

Davis had the better of it, with his rubicund exuberance. Both were prodigies of industry, but Mr. Davis knew how to play as he went along, while Mr. Coolidge did not. Outdoor sports, music, a gathering of Elks meant much to Mr. Davis, little to Mr. Coolidge. Mr. Davis, expansive, loquacious; Mr. Coolidge, silent, self-contained. They attained political success by opposite routes.

Mr. Coolidge represses emotions of exuberant geniality. If he has ever slapped any elector on the back or grabbed an extended human paw robustly with both hands, history makes no record thereof. Mr. Davis with unaffected pleasure pumps the elector's right hand, gives him social massage about the arms and shoulders, exudes solicitude for his health and happiness. He glows with pleasure when an acquaintance drops in and inquires, "What did you pay for that sporty necktie?" or "How does your corporosity sagaciate this bright morning?" Address such personal inquiries to Mr. Coolidge and he curls up within his shell like an exasperated armadillo.

It's all wrong, of course, to judge a man by external appearances, but on what philosophers call "the impression of the first look" the jocund and flawless countenance of Mr. Davis presents a striking contrast to the physiognomy of Mr. Coolidge.

To this day, Mr. Davis' face is as smoothly faultless as a perfect artificial pearl or a chromo of moonlight and roses done on linoleum.

"He was a man born with thy face and throat, Lyric Apollo!"

But success as a popular leader is not always a matter of personal pulchritude. Look at Mahatma Gandhi!

Mr. Davis is as fraternal as the starlings which congregate at nightfall in the nooks and crannies of the District Building on Pennsylvania Avenue, Washington. Mr. Davis is a grand mixer, with a gift for calling comparative strangers by first names.

If Mr. Coolidge has ever addressed casual friends by their first names, history shows no record of it. There are exceptions, of course, to every rule. The Honorable James B. Reynolds, former Assistant Secretary of the Treasury and unofficial political adviser to three Presidents, is universally known as Jimmie Reynolds. Jimmie enjoys the distinction of being addressed in Mr. Coolidge's delightful twang as "James." So does Jim Davis.

A schoolboy writing from Mooseheart, Illinois, addresses the Secretary of Labor as "My dear Jim." "Dear Jim" is able to call ten thousand Pennsylvania electors by their first names. This record probably is exceeded by no other man in public life, with the possible exception of Senator Watson, of Indiana.

Mr. Coolidge never joined any fraternal organization.

Mr. Davis, in his own words, says, "I am willing to join any fraternal society that will admit me and has for its purpose the good of mankind." It is not surprising, therefore, to find the name of Mr. Davis inscribed upon the parchment rolls of Baptists, Elks, Templars, Guernsey Cattle Breeders, Odd Fellows, Masons, Shriners, Tall Cedars of Lebanon, Kiwanis, Foresters, Rotarians, Maccabees, B'nai Briths, Artisans' Order of Mutual Protection, Amalgamated Association of Iron, Steel and Tin Workers of North America, Mystic Order of Veiled Prophets of the Enchanted Realm, Improved Order of Red Men, Knights of Pythias, Koran Grotto, Spanish War Veterans, Pittsburgh Boosters' Association, Loyal Order of Moose—of which he was director general—Eagles, Owls. His membership in the two later orders naturally carries ex-officio membership in all the Audubon Societies of America. Like Saint Francis of Assisi, Mr. Davis is little brother to the birds.

So put Mr. Davis down for membership in all sodalities, lodges, nests, temples, wigwams, grottoes, forests, dens and aviaries.

Membership in a lodge bolsters up a man's self-esteem and feeds the inner springs of confidence, thus stimulating him to noble emprise and valorous deeds of pith and moment.

Array a timid, obscure man in the regalia of an exalted potentate and you set his feet upon the ascending steps of infinite progression. What is wanted in this humdrum workaday life is liberation from the prison of reality into the ampler world of make-believe.

Mr. Davis is governed by his sympathies rather than his antipathies. He is a pro man rather than an anti man. God bless you, dear folks, one and all! What he is for would outrun the limits of our story, but certain things may be mentioned:

HE'S FOR:

The Flag
The Constitution
Ethics
Law
Order
Faith of the fathers
The Brotherhood of Man
The Ten Commandments
The Golden Rule

The protective tariff
The American home
American womanhood
American manhood
American childhood
Prosperity
Palladiums of Liberty
Divine gift of song
Shorter hours
More pay

He's Against:

| | |
|---|---|
| The Bolshies | Tribulation |
| The Wobblies | Sickness |
| The Reds | Poverty |
| Idleness | Sin |
| Low wages | |

Mr. Coolidge always kept about one lap ahead of Mr. Davis. He was getting himself elected city solicitor of the city of Northampton at the salary of sixty-five dollars a month just as Mr. Davis was getting himself chosen city clerk of Elwood at a salary of forty dollars a month. Mr. Coolidge at about the same era was wont to attire himself neatly, not to say nattily, in a suit of fair cut supported by a starched shirt and white collar. Mr. Davis contemporaneously was still in the hickory-shirt-and-blue-denim-overalls stage, with the white-collar-and-starched-shirt era yet to be. Mr. Davis' election to public office definitely transferred him sartorially to the white-collar class, though his sympathies just as definitely remained with the collarless of earth.

What we get out of this comparative method of study is the conclusion that there is a diversity of human talents, that we can't all be Leonardo da Vincis, and that one star differs from another star in glory.

The Psychological Method:

As a man thinketh in his heart, so is he. What does Mr. Davis think? We ought to know by this time, since for forty years he has been expressing himself copiously in the spoken and written word. Mr. Davis further expresses himself symphonically as a clarinet player and a sympathetic Welsh-ballad singer. When Mr. Davis bursts into Welsh song over a coast-to-coast radio hook-up, some persons unacquainted with the Welsh language set down the aerial disturbance to a bad case of static. The initiated know better. They recognize in Mr. Davis the best all-around Welsh song bird in America and one of the small group of songsters in the Western Hemisphere who can handle the Welsh vocable *"Llanfairpwllgwyngyllgogerychwyrndrobdllllandysiliogogogoch"* without coming up for air. Though he has no great fund of small talk, he's willing to talk about small matters. He's sincerely interested in people and their problems. He'll listen attentively to trifling talk of inconceivable unimportance. He likes men and enjoys mixing with them. About the only human types he doesn't mix freely with are drunkards, idlers and professional trouble-makers.

"Some men are by nature beavers," he tells us, "some are rats. The beaver is a builder, the rat is a destroyer, yet they both belong to the rodent race. I boast of beaver blood in my veins."

No idle boast! Mr. Davis has worked like a beaver all his life. As to the Reds who believe in leveling down, he looks upon them as aberrations from the kindly race of normal men. Some theorists look upon criminality as a disease. Mr. Davis looks upon communists as sick men.

"Communists," he tells us, "are tired men. What they need is a dose of castor oil. I never knew a communist in my life that was a well man."

This philosophy, of course, endears Mr. Davis to a considerable class of persons who cherish the inviolability of property rights. Mr. Davis has this much in common with Voltaire, who declared that "all people are good except those who are idle."

Mr. Davis' celerity in getting ahead in the world is largely due to his habits of industry. He is thoroughly alive—alive in every pore and with every muscle and brain cell aching for activity. Mr. Davis' philosophy of life is largely built upon a foundation of physical robustness. To Mr. Davis, the common physical ills, such as pyorrhea, sinus trouble, granulated eyelids, fallen arches, obstreperous adenoids, backfiring tonsils, are but empty names. They no more touch his life than does the seven-year itch that disturbed the peace of the early Manchu monarchs. Exuberant physical well-being—how few possess it, how many of us yearn for it!

As the most eupeptic and robustious of contemporary American social thinkers, Mr. Davis tells us that "good board consists of lots of greasy meats, strong coffee and slabs of sweet pie with gummy crust as thick as the palm of my hand. Nobody knows how to make pies but the American housewife. And lucky that she does, for men can not thrive in America without pie." Fate thus turns thumbs down on the writer, since it just happens that he can not eat pie, greasy meats, or drink strong coffee. Still there is some comfort in recalling such conspicuous pie abstainers as Erasmus, Julius Cæsar, Carlyle and Shelley who rose above the common ruck of humanity. His tribute to the American housewife as the world's pie-maker *par excellence* will be acclaimed by everybody with approval. Mr. Davis seldom misses an opportunity to pay a deserved tribute to the housewife.

In a recent radio hook-up, Mr. Davis' advertised subject was The Greatest Business Manager in the World. In withholding the identity of the manager referred to, Mr. Davis kept us all on the tenterhooks of dramatic suspense. Some put their money on Owen D. Young, others on Mussolini, others on Henry Ford. But all were wrong. Here is Mr. Davis' verdict:

"The greatest, busiest business executive in the world is the wife of the American working man. She keeps her youngsters well fed, happy and healthy because she is an economical purveyor, buyer and cook, one who knows how to save her husband's money, and who is lavish in her own thought and energy. Man's work is from sun to sun, but woman's work is never done from Sunday morning until Saturday night. That's the situation in a nutshell for our biggest, busiest business executive. This great country of ours may well be thankful that it has to its everlasting glory this wonderful element among us, the reverent, faithful, devoted, patient, hard-working, ennobling wife of our American working man."

Mr. Davis received bushels of complimentary letters from some of the millions of devoted women to whom just tribute was rendered, but, curiously enough, not one letter of appreciation was received from any husband.

"I have always regarded myself," writes Mr. Davis, "as a humorist, but the impression I made on my comrades was that of a serious and religious fellow."

Just an illustration or two of Mr. Davis' humor:

"I learned," writes he, "that blood is not only thicker than water but is thicker than curdled milk, and you can't line up a mother against her own children, even if you chased the cows until they got so wild that they gave strawberry pop instead of milk."

Again, he tells the story of how a white man came along and put a spoonful of quinine in the open mouth of a sleeping negro. The darky, awakened by the bitter taste, asked the white man what it all meant. "It means," informed the white man, "that you have done busted your gall and haven't long to live."

These humorous sallies, of course, get a big hand from any audience. It is only the literalists who are solemnized by Mr. Davis' humor. Despite every proof to the contrary, they still regard him as "a serious and religious fellow."

When he describes a puddling furnace as "hot as the Fourth of July in Abyssinia," everybody applauds the pat illustration save perhaps some literalist from Abyssinia, who points out that the country is one lofty plateau broken by snow-covered mountains, with July the rainiest, coldest and most shivery month of the year.

Speaking of the blessings of going shirtless in the terrific heat of a rolling mill, Mr. Davis humorously points his story with the remark:

"Adam enjoyed that blessing in the Garden of

Eden. And when he sinned they punished him by putting a shirt, collar and necktie on him."

"Keep working and you'll get the chromo," urges Mr. Davis. But some fastidious folk disdain chromos; they want oil paintings.

Mr. Davis rises to lyric enthusiasm when he dwells on the opportunities which America affords men of character and industry.

"My early days," he tells us, "were spent at forge and puddling furnace. The iron that I made is civilization's tools. I ride by night in metal bedrooms. I hear the bridges rumble underneath the wheels, and they are part of me. I see tall cities looking down from their iron heights upon me."

At forty he had amassed a sizable fortune. "This," he tells us, "gave me great confidence in myself and in the institutions of this country. A land where a boy can enter the mills at eleven, learn two trades, acquire a sound business education and make a competence in his thirties is not such a bad country."

"You'll never get anywhere, Jim," fellows used to say to Mr. Davis in his younger days, "as long as your conscience is so darn active. To win in this world, you've got to be slick." But Mr. Davis refused to be slick. That sort of thing is not in his make-up. As a harmonizer and pacifier he's smooth, but not slick. Put him down among a crowd of excited laboring men, all talking angrily at once, and it won't be long before he "takes the break," as the musicians say, and the ensemble chorus becomes a Davis solo.

Mr. Davis doesn't smoke, cuss, tipple, dice, lay wagers, bet on the ponies. He has no dissipation but work and service. But even here the word "dissipation," with its usual connotation of waste, is out of place. He no more wastes his energies than does a bit of radium which throws off emanations without lessening its bulk or impairing its value.

On one occasion, the Secretary of Labor intervened to prevent the deportation, on a technicality, of a God-fearing immigrant mother and her brood of healthy and right-minded children.

"I recalled to the mother that I had been one of such a family entering the port of New York some forty years before. Little did I dream then that I would ever be a member of a President's Cabinet, with power to wipe away this woman's tears and turn her heart's sorrowing into a song of joy. I told the mother that the baby in her arms might be Secretary of Labor forty years hence."

A touching incident, altogether creditable to our poor fallen humanity.

As director general of the Loyal Order of Moose, Mr. Davis saw that benevolent organization grow from a membership of two hundred forty-seven persons, including himself, to close on to seven hundred thousand. In his iron-puddling days it was the sad experience of Secretary Davis to witness family tragedies when accident or death crippled the chief breadwinner. He saw tiny children dispatched to orphan asylums.

Jim Davis' pity for the orphans of working men found practical expression in the establishment of the great institution of Mooseheart, Illinois, where Moose orphans are given a chance in life as former Congressman Vestal eloquently put it in his just eulogy of Secretary Davis on the floor of the House of Representatives: "To-night, in Mooseheart, one thousand four hundred children will kneel beside their trundle beds and say their prayers for a man who has made it possible for them to have a home and to receive an education that will fit them for the battles of life on even terms with the more fortunate children of America."

Varied and complex problems confront a Secretary of Labor. Immigration, naturalization, labor conciliation—it's enough to know that Mr. Davis' task, like that of "our greatest executive, the laboring man's wife," was never done. New forces of

Thirty years ago the Davises in Sharon, Pennsylvania, like the Coolidges in Northampton, Massachusetts, occupied the hither end of a double frame house

The Davis Washington home, next door to the new British Embassy, is big enough to accommodate a baby blimp

thought and feeling sweep the country. Constant readjustments must be made to meet the changed labor conditions of an ever-changing world. The old clean-cut oppositions between capital and labor no longer exist in this country. In the past decade, strikes and lockouts have consistently dwindled. There were about one-sixth as many in 1928 as ten years before. Organized labor has attained its objective of an eight-hour day and is now advancing toward the goal of a shorter week. The five-day week is already enjoyed by five hundred thousand organized workers. The distinction between capital and labor is blurring all the time.

Mr. Davis, representing the hosts of labor, is well fixed after a manner of speaking, with a huge stake in the efficient management of American business. Mr. Davis is implacably hostile to labor extremists as represented by the communist element. Thus it happens that the capitalists extend to the affluent Mr. Davis the right hand of fellowship, while organized labor finds in him a true and sympathetic friend. With respect to wages, he was as efficient as the flexible-tariff device in seeing to it that rates go up and by no misadventure come down. Wages held like a rock after the business sinking spell following last autumn's stock-market crash.

The old, crucial, industrial controversies are

# CHAPTER XI
## PRESIDENT PATTON

### DOCTOR SUBTILIS ET ANGELICUS

I CAN only set down what I know about Dr. Francis L. Patton, fourteen years President of Princeton University, from vivid, first-hand impressions. As undergraduate and postgraduate student, my Princeton contacts with Doctor Patton covered about one-half of his administration.

Doctor Patton came to us from west of the railroad station where in the Princeton Theological Seminary he occupied the Chair of the Relations of Philosophy and Science to the Christian Religion. It might have been the Chair of the Egypticity of the Pentateuch or Coptic Literature so far as we Princeton undergraduates knew or cared. An indefinable taint of ecclesiasticism clung to him. We were to be admonished, sermonized, disciplined after the John Knox fashion. With new currents of thought and feeling sweeping over Princeton it seemed a backward step to take a man with a white lawn tie, a black frock coat, side whiskers and the pallor of a medieval monk out of a theological seminary to preside over a college devoted chiefly to the liberal arts.

In Patton the Middle Ages seemed to live again—
he was the stern and subtle dialectician—Duns
Scotus (the Doctor Subtilis) redivivus after six
hundred years. But if he were the schoolman of
the cutting dialectic he was no less the human,
kindly Saint Thomas Aquinas, the Doctor Angel-
icus. Doctor Patton was indeed a theologian, but
of the three-dimensional type. His mental make-
up was a synthesis of intellect, feeling and will.
To look at him you would not suspect the hidden
depths of feeling. But we came to know those
depths. We came to know him as one of the fore-
most thinkers of the Anglo-Saxon world. But the
words which caused our hearts to burn while we
walked with him by the way sprang from a tender,
sympathetic understanding. Thinker, dialectician, logician—but something more than all this—
he was a man of deep feeling. Thus it was that his
thought often transcended logic. He found his
philosophy of life as a mystic finds his God in the
recesses of his own soul.

We misjudged him at first—underestimated
him. Coming to reign over us in the autumn of
1888 Princeton was still in a state of beatitude over
the magnificent football team which had overwhelmed Yale and Harvard the season before.
Early in the season the appalling rumor got around

like a corrupting miasma that our new president
was indifferent if not actively hostile to athletics.
From the undergraduate standpoint it looked as if
Princeton had got no bargain in Patton. Some
who knew gave him a character, as the saying is,
but so was the meddling, persecuting Archbishop
Laud a man of good character, while Torquemada,
Chief Inquisitor of the Holy Office, was a man of
blameless character who thought to render God
service by burning men alive who differed with
him on points of doctrine. Doctor Patton had to
earn his place; he had to win our affections. Like
the Great Apostle, he was a man of tact, and like
him he was in the best sense of the term all things
to all men. At any rate, having no taste for physical exercise, he made shift to attend football practise occasionally and put no curb on athletics. "If
we are not ourselves pious," reasoned the tolerant
Pope Julius II, "why should we prevent other
people from being so?"

I can remember with clear exactitude Doctor
Patton, pale of face in his tightly buttoned frock
coat, jostled by the throng of corduroy-trousered
and besweatered students on the varsity football
field, applauding with thin hands a goal kick from
the thirty-five-yard line. "Ye who strive after a
corruptible crown," he seemed to be saying, squint-

ing quizzically through gold-rimmed spectacles in the unaccustomed light of day. His head was carried high—as much through necessity as through pride. His poke collar impinged on the jugular threatening always to lacerate his neck—lacerate it severely. Back in the early 'nineties Doctor Patton offended no fashion in facial furbelows by the proliferation of thin side whiskers after the Lord Dundreary manner. But he developed as a crab grows by bursting its hard shell and casting it off. The collar came down in height, the more secular black tie supplanted the white tie for business wear. The austere side whiskers were shorn away. His thin cheeks filled out with the years and some said that traces of sun tan were discernible upon his pallid countenance. Nearing fifty, he took to smoking cigars. My classmate, Roy Goldsbury, calling on him a couple of years ago in his Bermuda home found him drawing on a rank black cigar *before* dinner.

This liberalization epoch followed the Briggs heresy trial which for months lay heavy upon him. It was perhaps the most distressing episode in his career. The fundamentals of the Christian religion were defended by him as a high-minded man would defend his personal honor. He preached a lofty morality and lived it. He was fundamentally the theologian but withal a humanist of deep and tender sympathies.

Endowed with deep sentiment he had no patience with sentimentality. One winter Princeton received a visit from the high-powered evangelist, Dr. Wilbur Chapman. A great student meeting was arranged by the visiting Doctor. The President of Princeton was notified by Doctor Chapman to be present.

"I shall not be there," Doctor Patton crisply responded. "I shall be in New York that evening whooping it up for Princeton at an Alumni Dinner." Doctor Chapman was sorely grieved and recorded an unfavorable opinion of Doctor Patton in a newspaper outgiving. Doctor Patton was an intensely spiritually minded man but he was devout rather than devotional. He hated cant and had no faith in modern rosewater devices for propagating the faith. How about the up-to-the-minute, four-square gospelers, the super-saccharine soul-savers? Evangels of the new gospel hedonism with conscience speaking in terms of "if" rather than in terms of "must," refining away even George F. Babbitt's pithily expressed ideas of retributive justice, "It stands to reason, boys, that you can't pull a lot of rough stuff in this world and not get nicked for it hereafter." Doctor

Patton has his opinions, no doubt, about the personable, white-robed hierophants of modern Mount Carmels, but he would be too considerate to express them.

When it was known that Doctor Patton was to preach in Marquand Chapel the compulsory chapel problem ceased to exist. The most indifferent of loafers slouched over to hear him. The appeal was to the heart as well as to the head. How many lectures, sermons or addresses do we remember clearly after forty years? The writer, with no memory to boast about, can reproduce in clear outline sermons of Doctor Patton listened to as an undergraduate. No rhetoric, no exaggeration—but a powerful appeal to the conscience and the intelligence. We of small capacity found ourselves confirmed in the faith by this great witness to the faith. If such a man, we reasoned, with his keen intellect and clear-eyed convictions accepted the "hard sayings" of supernaturalism why shouldn't we accept them on his authority?

If Doctor Patton was not a great scholar he was a great thinker and an inspiring teacher. Why is it that we men grown gray who listened to his words a generation ago still remember them clearly and are inspired to live by them, while the arid erudition which was crammed down our throats by pedants importantly busy about unimportant things has vanished like the empty fabric of a vision and left not a wrack behind? Doctor Patton was the great master in comparison with the schoolmasters who passed as scholars among the learned. What much of it was about I don't rightly understand to this day, but I do retain the impression that these arid scholars teaching learning's crabbed text would have made no great success if loosed in a hard competitive world, and that Doctor Patton would have made a brilliant success as a lawyer, physician, or writer of books.

Whatever his manifold capacity, he was not designed by nature to be a policeman. He would have failed altogether as a bureaucrat. Set him down in a faculty meeting to arbitrate some tedious routine matter, such as a proposed change of the lecture hour of Roman Law B-5, and you have the poet Shelley set down in a certified-cost-accountant's convention. Doctor Patton wanted to tighten up on discipline and the curriculum requirements, but it was a cart-horse job for which he was unfitted by taste, talent and experience. His native haunts were far out on the aerial boundaries of speculation and philosophy. His was not a nature to be clamped down by the weight of petty details or fed on the mean diet of compromise and routine.

He had no discipline in his own classroom. He didn't require any. His students were too eager to catch his great accents. But I do recall occasions where he turned aside in a half-amused, ironical way to rebuke inattention. When some students began shuffling their feet in anticipation of the close of the lecture hour Doctor Patton interjected with his quizzical smile: "Please restrain your impatience, I have still a few more pearls to cast." When a good-natured dullard fell asleep during a lecture on the free-will controversy Doctor Patton aroused him by demanding in a slightly treble, sonorous voice: "Mr. M, in permitting your mind to play over this complicated problem, do you align yourself with the determinists or the indeterminists?" "I haven't determined, Sir," answered the half-awake student. Nobody was more amused at the answer than Doctor Patton.

When a student on the back row interrupted the lecturer by shouting: "Please speak a little louder, Doctor, we can't understand you back here." "That's because you sit too far back, intellectually," countered Doctor Patton.

"On one occasion," explained Doctor Patton, "I called a student up after class and chided him for not taking notes on my lectures. It turned out that the student was deaf and attended the lectures only as a matter of form, using notes taken down by a classmate. Since then I have never rebuked a student for inattention in the classroom. I charitably assume that he's either deaf or dumb."

Doctor Patton, slightly annoyed by the voluble blurb of an ignorant student, quoted Tennyson:

"I do but sing because I must,
And pipe because the linnets do."

Doctor Patton had a faculty of extracting whimsical humor out of the commonplaces in life and somehow or other his wit never left a sting. Back of his wit lay a kindly twinkle of the eye, a twitching at the corners of the mouth. In one of his turnings aside to describe the efforts of the Prophet Nehemiah to rebuild the walls of Jerusalem he noted in the Scriptural narrative that some men were called to mix mortar, others to carry spears and shields, others to sound the trumpet. Applying the lesson to modern society he remarked that many a man could say when confronted by a difficult job: "I can't mix mortar, I can't carry the hod, I can't fight, but Lord I *can* blow."

"Doctor Patton," inquired a student, "how do you reconcile Biblical contradictions such as this— we are told in one chapter to answer a fool according to his folly and in another to answer not a fool according to his folly." "The seeming contradiction is explained," said Doctor Patton, "by the existence in this world of two kinds of fools, one type you may argue with, another you may not."

As an acute dialectician he had a way of compacting a deal of substance into a single sentence: "The behaviorists address books to the consciousness of their readers to prove there is no such thing as consciousness," or "France by a fierce action of replevin is snatching back from Germany her stolen provinces." It was characteristic of the good Doctor that he could rebuke and confound a man without hurting his feelings. As editor of the *Princetonian* I once wrote a philosophic editorial counseling the undergraduates to bear the sorrows of a football defeat like men and added the naïve observation that a great deal is still left us in this world, that "after all, we come to Princeton in the pursuit of learning." In chapel the next morning Doctor Patton had something to say about the two words "after all." He was cheered and helped in his ambitions to develop Princeton as a seat of learning by the words "after all," which implied to his mind a willingness on the part of the undergraduates to concede something to the cause of a liberal education.

Doctor Patton had five sons of whom the eldest,

George, was a classmate of mine. The occasional dinners with the Pattons were always delightful. Everybody was on a conversational level—freedom of speech prevailed. One evening at dinner Bob Patton, a pleasant, brown-faced boy who still had a career to make in the world, remarked that any girl who got him would have to be liberally endowed with three b's—brains, beauty, bullion. "And you, I suppose," interjected Doctor Patton, "will compensate her amply by furnishing one b—Bob."

The whole life of the college was infused with the personality of Doctor Patton just as the *New York Sun* for years bore the impress of Dana's personality on its news and editorial columns. Princeton in the Golden 'Nineties was run on the *laissez-faire* principle. One could spell it, I suppose, "lazy fare." Life was easy-going, slack, the proportion of loafers large. Doctor Patton met the loafer issue in his whimsical way by entering the lawyer's plea of confession and avoidance. Paraphrasing Tennyson, he remarked of the college idlers and dilettantes,

"It's better to have come and loafed
Than never to have come at all."

Still, Princeton was a world of teeming activities. Interest was intense in public debating and

Doctor Patton as he is to-day

Oval insert:  Doctor Patton in the clerical garb and proliferation of
side whiskers common some forty years ago

oratorical contests. An efflorescence of literary effort centered about the *Nassau Lit.* It was the era when Booth Tarkington, James Barnes, Jesse Lynch Williams, Howard Crosby Butler, Lansing Collins, Jesse Benedict Carter, in obedience to the larval instinct, were thrusting upward to the light. In an intensely democratic, comradely community the college spirit burned in passionate loyalty to Princeton, the like of which has not been seen since, either in Princeton or in any other college. Later the student body becoming big in numbers and dignified in deportment took the road to decorous dullness.

My classmate, Gordon Murray, is wont to refer to the Golden 'Nineties as Princeton's Age of Pericles. It's like eating one's cake and having it, too, to expect the Age of Pericles to be regimented and standardized after the Spartan fashion. You can't have a Doctor Patton and a red-blooded, hustling George Babbitt all in one.

Doctor Patton was endowed with the God-given power to sit. Physically he was indolent, dilatory. He bore no grudges, cared nothing for money, power or place, and in consequence was not embittered by frustrations. He never attained the lofty heights of his successor but he lived a happier man—and he still lives. Yes, he was a man of contemplation, content to sit, to live comfortably with himself, to range the capacious chambers of his own mind. He reminds one in his sitting attitude of the carven images of sitting men before the Temple of Abu Simbel in the Nile Valley—motionless figures that sit with indolent hands upon their knees, staring inscrutably and, it seems, with a faint trace of ironic interest, into the void. The great metaphysician Kant was never, in a long life, more than fifty miles from his quiet home. Modern science is the product of men who are content to sit still in a room and with microscope and test tube challenge the mysteries of the universe. Doctor Patton would sit for hours in his study grasping a cologne scented handkerchief in his thin hands. Occasionally he would lay down the handkerchief, take up a pen, and make a few calligraphic scratches on a sheet of paper. He hated the manual labor of writing and would often add the completing touches to a sermon during the singing of the second hymn. He ordinarily began a discourse with his handkerchief clutched tight in his right hand. Back of every spoken word seemed to lie a vibrant intellectual vitality which carried the words of the speaker in high-pitched, sonorous tones to his remotest hearers.

What he needed, or rather what the world

needed for him, was an unobtrusive Boswellian stenographer to ply him with questions and set down his words for posterity. We petty writers, incurably obscure, and with money hard to come by, labor with our pens to feed the ego and redress mayhap an unfavorable bank balance. But Doctor Patton was not so goaded. He cared nothing for fame or money, hated the sight of a pen. He bequeaths to posterity two or three books of a religiophilosophic character and a few gem-like addresses such as his poignantly beautiful tribute to his dead friend, Dr. Caspar Wistar Hodge.

After fourteen years Doctor Patton found himself unequal to the task of being what in the beginning we foolishly feared he was, namely, a high-powered executive. He unexpectedly submitted his resignation and along with it a recommendation that Professor Woodrow Wilson should be chosen in his stead. Mr. Ray Stannard Baker, official Wilson biographer, remarks: "Behind the rejoicing over Woodrow Wilson's election to the presidency of Princeton lay deep the feeling amongst those who knew and loved Princeton that the institution had ceased making progress under the leadership of President Patton and that with Wilson in command it would at once take on new life."

## DATE DUE